KANVASHRAM – A LOST HERITAGE

Birth Place of Emperor Bharat and Vedic Culture

Lt. Commander Virendra Singh Rawat (R'etd)
Indian Navy

Clever Fox®
PUBLISHING
Chennai • Bangalore

CLEVER FOX PUBLISHING
Chennai, India

Published by CLEVER FOX PUBLISHING 2025

ISBN: 978-93-340-1506-5

To our ancestors who bestowed upon us the wisdom and knowledge to grasp the profound intricacies of nature and the universe

CONTENTS

PROLOGUE

The book being presented is an attempt to convey to the people of this ancient nation and the world about an overlooked fragment of a glorious ancient heritage of a nation, called *Bharat Varsh*. A subcontinent integrated and unified for the first time as a nation by Emperor Bharat, son of King Dushyant and Shakuntala. With the flow of time, though the nation created as Bharat Varsh, retained its identity and boundaries, the name itself was lost and surprisingly went out of usage. Not only the name, strangely all the historical details and events connected with the creator of this nation, somehow disappeared. No information is available in any of the ancient history books, written by eminent historians of this nation, about the period of reign of Emperor Bharat and neither is there any documented information available about the social, cultural, economic or political conditions which prevailed during his reign. The nation created by Emperor Bharat continued to prosper after his death and achieved great heights in various fields, which included language, mathematics, science, astronomy, astrology, agriculture, spirituality etc. but inexplicably though the reference to its creator, does not find mention in ancient documents, except a few.

Sometimes, between the dawn of civilisation on this huge land mass, which blossomed along the bank of river Sarasvati and long before the great war of Mahabharat, fought between brothers, on the battlefield of Kurukshetra, a child was born, who was brought up in an *ashram* situated on the bank of river Malini. It was the *ashram* of *rishi* Kanv. The *ashram* was known as Kanvashram. It was the first Vedic education, cultural and spiritual centre of repute in this subcontinent, where hundreds if not thousands of students toiled to acquire knowledge. Kanvashram was in fact the first university established on this planet Earth. This subcontinent at that juncture was referred to as *Arya Vrat*, a place where *Arya* resided. *Arya* is a word that defines a human in Sanskrit, as the best or perfect or possibly both. It is a word, like many other words, which have no parallel word in the English language. The child brought up in Kanvashram subsequently grew up and became a mighty Emperor. With his velour, courage and foresight he unified this huge stretch of land, for the very first time, into a nation and ruled it for many years. He was called भरत (Bharat). Many centuries and many generations later, it was his descendants who fought the great war, described in the world's largest ancient epic Mahabharat. The war was fought for possession of land and resources. The two armies, consisting of elephants, chariots, horsemen and foot soldiers clashed on the battlefield of Kurukshetra. Presently a town Kurukshetra, exists in the state of Haryana, India. Kurukshetra was a vast region, which was located south of the disappearing ancient river Sarasvati, though by then with reduced flow, Sarasvati was still flowing in that region. For it was on the banks of river Sarasvati, where the earliest human civilisation in this world took root and blossomed, sometime before 10,000 BCE. Though extinct, river Sarasvati was the mightiest of all rivers, which ever flowed on this subcontinent. The story of river Sarasvati's disappearance is as fascinating and captivating, as the disappearance from history, of all references about Emperor Bharat and Kanvashram. Numerous kings along with their powerful armies fought this battle, from either side. Details of the battle and events leading to the ultimate conflict, between Pandav and Kaurav, are described in the minutest of details, in Mahabharat. The kingdom of the rulers who fought the great war stretched from present-day countries like Afghanistan, Pakistan to states in India like Rajasthan, Haryana, Punjab, Uttar Pradesh and Jammu & Kashmir.

As the years went by, the nation *Bharat Varsh* created by Emperor Bharat became a prosperous nation. With its immense wealth, the nation was designated the title of **सोने की चिडिया** (A Golden Bird), implying a land full of riches. Taking all factors into account, the primary reason that attributed to the prosperity of Bharat Varsh, was a stable social and climatic condition in the region, which helped in the development of agriculture, trade, culture and ultimately educational and spiritual activities. The presence of such immense wealth in this nation did not go unnoticed by its neighbours, living in poverty, lying to the west of this nation. Attracted by the riches and knowledge, primarily the former, of this prosperous nation, plunderers, looters and invaders from far-flung regions headed towards this nation, to somehow reach this promised land. Most came by land via present-day Afghanistan but some like Vasco-da-Gama, reached following Indian traders, who have been navigating the sea routes in the Indian Ocean to Africa, since time immemorial. Amongst the earliest recorded looter and plunderer was a Greek named Alexander. He managed to reach the western bank of river Sindhu (Indus) in 326 BCE, the outer boundaries of this nation. His further progress into the nation Bharat Varsh was halted by the rulers of kingdoms, lying on the fringes of this nation. Most armies of these rulers were equipped with war-hardened elephants, an animal the Greeks had never seen before. In the ensuing battles, Alexander lost most of his army, which was completely decimated. His remaining soldiers refused to fight and revolted. They were fortunate not to have faced the army of the ruler of this nation, Nand dynasty (345–322 BCE). A great military power, having a force thousands of times greater than that of the Greeks. The capital of their kingdom was Maghad but the boundaries of their empire extended up to river Sindhu. Some regions west of river Sindhu continued to be under the control of Greeks, even after the flight of Alexander from the region. The Greeks were ultimately driven out by Chandragupt Maurya, who overthrew the Nand dynasty in 322 BCE. He ruled from 324 to 301 BCE and was the architect of the first imperial power in this subcontinent. His capital Patliputra, is described as a magnificent city of temples, universities, libraries and gardens.

On the other hand, traders, travellers, and explorers from distant lands reached the shores of this nation, to seek educational and spiritual knowledge. All such visitors were welcomed with open arms. Some stayed on forever, while others returned, having gained a huge quantum of knowledge, in various fields. A Greek historian and explorer who visited Patliputra, wrote about this nation, in his famous memoirs, a book called Indica. In his book he described a society, which existed in the nation Bharat Varsh, far advanced in cultural, educational, social and spiritual values. Besides him two other, prominent Chinese travellers also visited this nation. Fi- Hian from 399 to 413 CE and Hewn Thang from 629 to 645 CE. They travelled widely across this nation before returning with loads of information and manuscripts to their nation. Besides all the documented information the visitors took with them, they also carried the message and concept of **विश्व कुटुम्बकम**, a message of universal brotherhood. An idea, a thought or a message necessary to maintain harmony and peace, amongst all those living on Mother Earth. This ideology of universal brotherhood still exists in this nation and is presently spreading worldwide.

Detailed description of their visit, written by the visitors, is a rich source of information about the prevailing situation in this nation.

Visitors, travellers, traders and invaders have been coming to this nation on regular intervals, each with their own ulterior motive. On reaching the shores of this nation, they were confronted with a complex and advanced language. Not having similar-sounding alphabets in their language, they designated new names to this nation. Ironically the new names given to this nation are still in popular usage. Due to this, the subcontinent came to be addressed by two new names, India and Hindustan. The nation finally unshackled itself from the grasp of colonial rule in 1947. The Constitution of this nation promulgated on 26 Jan 1951, also for some inexplicable reason, adopted the name designated to this nation by the colonial ruler and it was officially adopted post-independence. The constitution of this nation starts with "INDIA that is BHARAT, shall be a union of states…" Possibly implying that the nation is to be called India, can also be addressed as Bharat. The elected representative at that time did not designate to this land its ancient name Bharat Varsh. They found Bharat unsuitable and gave preference to India, a name used by the colonial ruler of this nation, which was derived from the word Indika or Indica given by the Greeks. At present, oddly, after 78 years of independence, this subcontinent Bharat Varsh continues to be addressed by names given to it by foreigners.

Hindustan, a name created due to a pronunciation paradox of the font of the language, by Arabs who visited this nation for trade and India given by the colonial rulers. The latter is extremely popular and the former given by the Arabs also commands a large usage. With no S in their language, the Arabs replaced S in Sindhu with H and called the people living across the river Sindhu as Hindu. With the same logic, they called the region as Hindustan. The word is made of two words Hindu and *Stan*. *Stan* in the Hindi language means a place or a region. Greeks romanised the word Sindhu and named the river Sindhu as Indus. They designated the place across the river Indus as Indica or Indika. The Greek name was further twisted by the Britisher and a new word India was created.

Civilisation took root in the Indian subcontinent, prior to the warming period, which commenced with the ending of the last mini-ice age in ~20,000 BCE. Long before the Pyramids came into existence in the desert of Egypt on the bank of river Nile or civilisation on the bank of river Tigris and Euphrates. No culturally developed civilisation existed anywhere else in this world, when cities and settlements flourished with thousands of inhabitants on this subcontinent, on the banks of river Sarasvati. The civilisation which came into existence then has continued unabated till date. Sadly though, this peaceful culturally and spiritually developed civilisation was attacked time and again by foreign invaders. Many years of occupation by foreign forces and plundering by the colonial ruler, destroyed a colossal amount of written and structural material of this nation. Most invaders concentrated on looting and carting away the material wealth of this nation but others inflicted greater damage by destroying thousands of libraries, religious and cultural sites spread all over this vast nation. Some just picked up and took away anything they found, not really knowing its true worth. Fortunately, the quantum of material present in the nation Bharat Varsh, was so immense and spread over such a vast area, that it was not humanly possible to cart away all or destroy it completely. A steady stream of fresh research about the depth of the civilisation of this subcontinent is gradually emerging and being released continuously by archaeologists, historians, independent writers and organisations in the form of research papers, articles, books etc. Citizens of this nation now have unrestricted access to explore and excavate any location within this nation's boundaries. After hundreds of years, the true and authentic history of this nation is being revealed. What has been presented as the history of this nation, till today by the unlawful occupiers of this land, was biased and a distorted view of this ancient nation. All this was primarily done to demean this nation, for political and social consideration. The researcher scholars of this nation and independent organization now appear to be on an overdrive, to ensure that the factual image and ancient heritage of this nation, Bharat Varsh, is unveiled speedily and presented in its true form, to the coming generations and the world. The preliminary results received, have already taken the origin of the civilisation in this region many thousands of years back into the past, from the false and dubious assessment made by European Indologists. In this long period of turmoil in this subcontinent, my effort is confined, to uncover one aspect of the hidden past of this nation. A period that lies prior to the great war of Mahabharat and after the disappearance of the river Sarasvati.

Carved stone pieces of ancient monuments have been found scattered over a vast area in a region, close to the town of Kotdwara in Uttarakhand, India, close to the bank of river Malini, where as per ancient scriptures, Kanvashram was located. The relics appear to be part of a building or may be of a religious structure. No one is definite about, as no official study or excavation has been undertaken by the government or any non-government organisation. However, as per a brief report prepared by the Archaeological Survey of India, Dehradun in 2012, submitted by them the relics have been sculptured between 10th and 12th CE. This was the period when many colossal and magnificent temples were constructed in this nation. Though most of the temples or religious sites still exist in Southern India, majority of those in the North, have either been destroyed or converted into other religious structures. The process of restoring these destroyed religious sites and educational institutes has commenced and in due course of time, they shall all once again shine in their original glory.

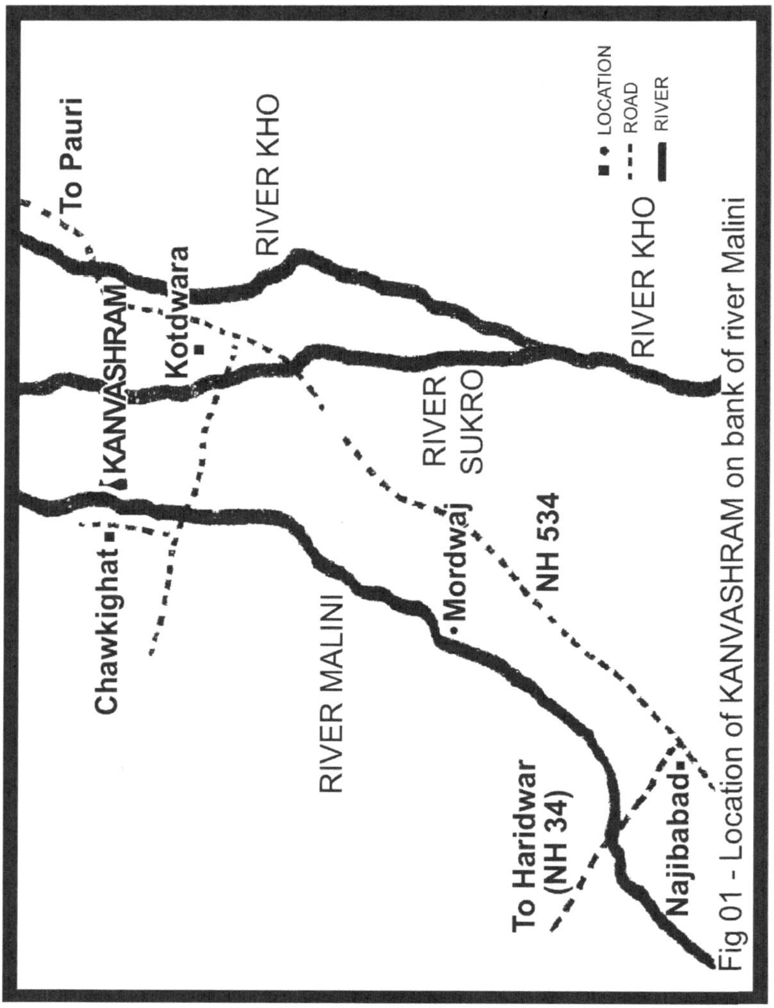

Fig 01 - Location of KANVASHRAM on bank of river Malini

Focus of my book is confined to the history of Kanvashram. An ancient heritage site that was not marked on any map produced or printed in this nation or anywhere in the world. Though, with the present technology it is possible to locate it on a digital map. The location of Kanvashram has now been affixed by Kanvashram Vikas Samiti, an NGO, which has been active since 1956, in promoting and making a dedicated effort, to bring to light, a part of the long-lost and forgotten heritage of this nation. Kanvashram is a region situated around a tiny hamlet Chawkighat, on the bank of river Malini, about 14 km from the town of Kotdwara in district Pauri Garhwal, Uttarakhand, India. **(Figure 01)** Somewhere along the bank of the river Malini, the creator of this nation Emperor Bharat, son of Shakuntala and King Dushyant was born and brought up in the ashram of *rishi* Kanv. A tantalizing and exciting love story of King Dushyant and Shakuntala, woven by the great poet and dramatist Kalidas, was captured and converted into a classical literary drama Abhigyan Shakuntalam. This literary masterpiece of Kalidas has been translated into more than 60 languages worldwide and drama composed and enacted in numerous nations in their respective languages. Kanvashram occupies a central and dominant position in the history of this nation. For it was Kanvashram which was at the cradle of cultural, spiritual and academic values of this nation, during that period. Kanvashram is akin to a glow of a dazzling flame, which spread the light of knowledge, to the world and to the complete human civilisation. Many civilisations have flourished in different regions and periods in the past, on this planet. Most are identified and credited with achievements in the form of monuments and burial structures remains, which can still be seen around. However, the only civilisation which gave knowledge, in numerous fields, to humanity for its future development, in the form of numbers, astronomy, science, agriculture etc., existed in this subcontinent called Bharat Varsh. In the forefront of dissemination of this knowledge was Kanvashram.

I shall confess at this stage that I am neither a historian nor an archaeologist. I consider myself fortunate to be residing in the region close to Kanvashram. After retirement from active duty as an aeronautical engineer in the Indian Navy, I settled in my ancestral village in 1992, to pursue the age-old tradition of farming. Though I was aware of the existence of a symbolic memorial of Kanvashram, built here, in 1956, by the government of Uttar Pradesh, indicating the presence of Kanvashram, on the banks of river Malini, I had no further knowledge of the history of the place or the place of Kanvashram, in the history of this nation. However, curiosity got the better of me and I ventured into the field of ancient history, a subject totally out of my field of vision. What brief knowledge I acquired about Kanvashram and its historical importance is based on my three decades of exploration and is being presented in the succeeding pages of this book. The subject being addressed is vast and uncharted.

It is like an uncoiled rope with its strands scattered all over and some strands not even existing. Limited information is available on the subject, as nothing has been penned down by historians of the bygone era. I am still determined and attempting to bring to light, what little I have learnt about the existence of the ashram of *rishi* Kanv, with a belief that the strands left unwoven are found by the coming generation and ultimately woven into an unbreakable rope.

I had a compulsive dislike towards history as a subject in school for reasons still not clear to me, but time and circumstances changed my perception towards history. Awareness about Kanvashram became a source of inspiration to me. As I dug into its past, I became aware of its links with the history of this nation. Historical data available today has gaping holes in it that leave a number of questions unanswered. Most of the historical information available in different ancient history books of this nation presents identical data with minor variations in language. It, in a way, appears to be copy and paste. Blanks have been left in the presentation of ancient history of this nation by historians and no effort was made to research or investigate and fill in the blanks. Kanvashram is one such subject, on which no historian, as per my knowledge ventured, to uncover the truth, as no straightforward evidence was available. In the succeeding pages, an effort is being made to uncover the history of Kanvashram and its link with the Vedic civilisation which prevailed in this nation, when Rig Veda was composed.

My exposure to the history of this nation via various ancient history books written by eminent historians educated me a lot, but somehow, I was quite surprised by the omission of some major events and prominent personalities, who had lived in this subcontinent, in the past. It was as if these people did not exist. The reason for ignoring these personalities and omitting this period of history was unclear to me. What is most amazing is that no one has even made an intelligent guess about that period and the events that took place therein. It is as if nothing existed or happened during that period. A complete millennium has somehow been erased from ancient history books without a trace. Starting from the displacement of people of Saraswati-Sindhu civilisation from ~2300 BCE to the occurrence of the great war described in Mahabharat, which happened between 1100 and 1200 BCE, no concrete information is available. No archaeological exploration or analysis of events in that time frame has been undertaken by historians, to fill in the blanks of the history of this nation. All this can be attributed to the fact that the educated masses of this nation were mesmerised by the Western historians, who convinced them that their ancestors were illiterate and ignorant, and never kept any historical records. The real reason behind non-availability of historical data was hidden from them and it was therefore impossible for them to know, when what happened, during that millennium. The questions which came to the fore are, how culturally weak or strong these people were, who lived in this subcontinent during that period and what relation they had with the nation Bharat Varsh. There are many questions that need answers. However, it is an extremely difficult task to fill in the gaps, in the ancient history of this nation, due to systematic destruction of ancient documents, books and literature in the last millennium by the barbaric invaders, who besides plundering this nation also destroyed and burnt all written literature, present in various libraries and universities. It is for this very reason that no documentary evidence is available. However, the period of history I am interested in was not found by me in any of the history books available in this nation. Quite intriguing?

Most of the ancient history books written generally begin by addressing this subcontinent as Bharat Varsh. Further, no other information is given in these books about the nation Bharat Varsh or its creator. So, it is now time to proceed to find out all about Emperor Bharat. This search, truly and logically should start by learning more about Emperor Bharat and the nation he created, which leads us to the place of his birth Kanvashram, a place where Vedic culture in this subcontinent originated. To locate and piece together the scattered strands of the rope is a challenge but then someone has to do it.

INTRODUCTION

Geographical description of this great and ancient nation Bharat Varsh, which stretches from the majestic snow-covered Himalayas in the North to the mighty Indian Ocean to its South, is aptly described in a *shlok* in *Vishnu Puran*, an ancient epic of this nation, written about a couple of thousand years ago.

उत्तरं यत् समुद्रस्य, हिमाद्रेश्चैव दक्षिणम् ।

वर्षम् तद् भारतम् नाम, भारती यत्र सन्ततिः

Lying North of the mighty ocean and South of the snow-covered mountains is a nation named Bharat Varsh, whose inhabitants are the descendants of Bharat(भरत). The *shlok* in Sanskrit has been invariably quoted in the first few pages of most ancient history books in circulation in this nation, written by eminent historians. However, no further information is given in any of these books, about the nation Bharat Varsh nor any reference to its ruler Bharat. Neither is there any information about his reign or any mention of economic, cultural or social conditions which prevailed in his kingdom. The extent of boundaries of his nation also finds no reference anywhere. Emperor Bharat, the creator of this nation Bharat Varsh, in simple words, has been ceremoniously put aside for reasons unknown. To know more about this huge subcontinent called Bharat Varsh, in the right perspective, it is necessary to go back in time to when it all began.

The geographical alignment of the land mass of the world as we see today, came into being very recently. It can be considered recent when compared with the age of the planet Earth being ~4.5 billion years. The present configuration of the continents formed about 50–55 million years ago. As per geologists, there existed a supercontinent that broke up due to tectonic movement of the earth's crust about 180 million years ago. This supercontinent was called Gondwana. Breaking up of the supercontinent released a land mass in the form of an island. A major event occurred when this drifting island collided with the Euro-Asian plate. The collision set forth a series of events, which ultimately culminated in the development of the most advanced civilisation on this drifting island, now a subcontinent. Creeping at snail's pace in a North North-East direction for about ~100 million years, this island travelled a great distance, before it ultimately collided with the Euro–Asian plate. After the initial contact, this huge land mass continued to push further and created the longest and greatest mountain range, now known to us as Himalayas. The formation of the youngest and highest mountain range on the planet created a new weather pattern in the region. About 10 million years ago, a periodic yearly cycle of rain in the region commenced, now referred to as Monsoon. Numerous glaciers formed in the mountain ranges of the Himalaya. Ending of the last mini-ice age and warming of planet Earth commenced in ~20,000 BCE, but its physical effect on ground became noticeable from ~11500 BCE onwards. The warming increased the quantum of meltwater discharged from the glaciers into the numerous rivers flowing in this subcontinent. The enormous amount of water received by the rivers drenched the vast plains of this subcontinent. Water rich in minerals and soil carried from the mountain was deposited on the northern plain region. Abundance of water, with a stable climatic, created conditions suitable for sustainable agriculture and gave rise to a new civilisation, which came up on the banks of river Sarasvati. For it was river Sarasvati and its tributaries, on whose banks, most of the human settlements of this civilisation have been found. The present number of settlements excavated till date is 4856, with 80% of these located in India.

At the time of the collision, no humans existed anywhere on our planet, though numerous animal and plant species did. As per anthropologists, a tree-dwelling animal climbed down leaving his natural safe abode in the tree, to venture onto the ground. The time was ~70 million years ago. This animal, which took to the ground and ultimately stood up on its two hind legs, was our earliest ancestor. The place or region where this happened cannot be pinpointed but as per current research, it occurred somewhere in Africa. Evolution took control thereafter and Homo Sapiens the present human being came into existence.

I have started from the very beginning, as I would like to link up the origin of the human, with the growth and development of the civilisation, in the subcontinent called Bharat Varsh. The earliest fossil of the creature which walked upright on two legs, has been discovered in Africa. Having evolved thousands of kilometres away, how did our ancestors manage to reach this sub-continent? Though the movement across the continents on foot seems impossible presently. Our ancestors were able to journey across the continents, to different places, as Earth periodically goes through major and mini-ice ages. The occurrence of these ice ages results in covering of a large portion of the earth in a thick sheet of ice. Over the past 100,000 years, Earth has experienced several mini–ice ages, driven by a variety of factors that both trigger and end these deep freezes. Drop in temperature causes a major portion of the water present on the planet to freeze in mountains, glaciers and poles. Reduction in free water results in a drop in the level of oceans. Before the commencement of present warming from ~20,000 BCE, the ocean level was about ~120 meters lower than where it is now. The fall in the level of oceans, during that period uncovered the coastal land. This connected the continents and it was possible to move between them.

The newly created land routes due to glaciation helped our wondering ancestors to migrate out of Africa, looking for favourable living conditions. They must have spread in all directions. Some who migrated eastward reached this subcontinent. Those who settled on the banks of river Sarasvati were fortunate and found conditions suitable in terms of stable weather conditions, with abundant availability of water. As the warming continued, the sea level rose and the exposed land routes were submerged under the rising oceans. The sea level we see today is marginally higher than what it was in 6000 BCE when the warming period ended. Yearly flooding of the region by river Sarasvati, deposited fresh mineral-rich soil in the region. With a regular yearly rain cycle in the region, it was possible for the settlers to grow different crops. The settlements of the migrants gradually expanded in the region along the bank of other rivers like Drishadvati, Sutlej, Sindhu etc. **(Figure 02).** Highly advanced ways of living have been observed in cities and settlements found in these regions. The settlers achieved great heights in various fields, gained knowledge about metallurgy and brought into use various metals. They became masters in manufacturing various items and excavating precious stones including diamonds and traded ornaments made of them. The ornaments crafted out of these precious stones in the Saraswati-Sindhu civilisation have been found in many adjoining regions.

British engineers involved in the construction of a rail track between Karachi and Lahore in 1856, were looking for a source of stones to lay as track ballast were directed by locals to a heap of bricks lying in a mound. Taking the bricks to be part of some old abandoned building, the

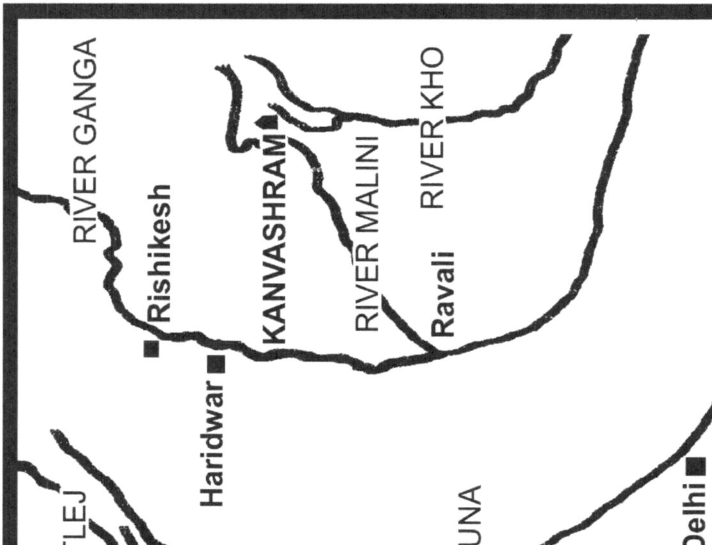

Fig 02 - River Sarasvati and river Malini

engineer instructed the labourers to break the bricks and use them as track ballast. The engineers were not aware that the abandoned dilapidated structures were the remains of one of the many settlements of the ancient Saraswati-Sindhu civilisation. The settlement unearthed was named Mohenjo Daro. As it was lying close to the river Indus the civilisation was called Indus Valley Civilisation (IVC). A large part of the ruins of the settlement was destroyed by the rail company. Alexander Cunningham, Director General of Archaeological Survey of North India, also visited the site. It was only in the early 20th century, when Indian archaeologists visited the area, that the true extent of the site was understood and serious research work was undertaken. As per the present finds and reckoning by a leading archaeologist of India, Saraswati- Sindhu civilisation was in existence centuries before from what has been assumed by Western historians. The dates of commencement of the civilisation have now been pushed back from 3000 to 7500 BCE, in view of the new find in Rakhigarhi, Haryana, India.

Of the many settlements, excavated partially or completely along the Saraswati, Drishadvati, Sutlej and other minor rivers, indicate that the civilisation blossomed at a gradual pace. In time, it spread over an extremely large area, with some major and many minor settlements. Majority of the remains of the civilisation unearthed are located in present-day Haryana, Punjab, Rajasthan and Gujrat in India. Then in a short period of time, the inhabitants of this most advanced civilisation on the planet abandoned their settlements. What caused the exodus? All research done on this calamity, points in one direction, that the reduction in availability of water in the region led to its disintegration. Sounds strange, that the mighty Sarasvati, whose banks at some stretches are estimated to be about 8 to 10 km apart, as mapped from satellite imagery, lost all its water. A glacial river fed by melting ice, topped up by yearly monsoon rain which had Sutlej, Jamuna, Drishadvati and many other rivers feeding into it, as its tributaries, became devoid of water. The loss of water from river Sarasvati is attributed by most, to geological changes due to tectonic upheavals and changes in meteorological conditions in the region. These events occurred concurrently over a short span of time, which caused the river Sarasvati to disappear from the face of the earth. It is one of the greatest mysteries of this planet, which has now been solved with the help of modern technological tools available and the dedicated efforts of eminent geologists and archaeologists. Where did the inhabitants of this well-entrenched and mature civilisation, spread over such a vast area migrate to? In the succeeding pages, I will not account for all the inhabitants, as they scattered in all directions, but confine myself to a small group of people, who after abandoning their settlement, on the bank of river Sarasvati, moved in an Easterly direction. Some of these migrants travelled a considerable distance and settled on the bank of a small insignificant river, flowing down from the Shivalik mountain range, in the state of Uttarakhand, India. A tributary of the mighty river Ganga, the settlers were aware of or became aware of rivers like Ganga and Jamuna, having crossed them to reach the bank of this small river. Though both rivers Ganga and Jamuna have a sumptuous flow of water, throughout the year, the migrants did not pitch their tents on their banks. They instead choose river Malini, whose flow is many times less. The migrants in the succeeding few centuries added many new chapters to the book of knowledge of human civilisation, which guided and moulded the educational, social, cultural and spiritual fabric of this subcontinent and the world. Educational institutes were established by them. The education system created continued to flourish in this nation for centuries thereafter. Following the stipulated guidelines, a number of educational centres and universities were established in this nation. Foreign invaders who penetrated the boundaries of this nation destroyed most of these educational centres. Major institutions like Nalanda, Takhshila etc., were demolished and razed to the ground. Not satisfied with killing the academic staff, the invaders burned the universities, possessing millions of manuscripts and the precious asset of this nation was lost forever.

There is not much geological or archaeological evidence available at hand to authenticate the presence and achievements of the people who settled on the banks of river Malini. With keen observation and vision, the settlers along the bank of river Malini gathered a vast quantum of information. The knowledge gained over hundreds of years, was passed orally from one generation to the next and was ultimately penned down in hand-written manuscripts. A name that surfaces in some of these ancient scriptures is Kanvashram. It is described as an educational and spiritual centre, which subsequently became a religious hub and was located on the banks of river Malini. No further information is available. The leads were limited and most often ended in a dead end. Are there some hidden reasons, to sidestep the subject or ignore the very existence of Kanvashram? I am not aware of any and would not like to speculate but I have a feeling that something is amiss. Some stumbled unknowingly about its presence like me. Others made a dedicated effort to uncover this lost heritage site. The two sources which gave some information about the existence of Kanvashram are Mahabharat and Abhigyan Shakuntalam. The former is the largest epic in the world containing 1,00,000 *shloks* and the second is the brilliant literary drama written by renowned dramatist Kalidas. Some references to Emperor Bharat and Bharat Varsh are also found in *Puranas*. In the current era, Kanvashram was recognized as a religious site, though its importance had faded with the coming of the Mughals and subsequently the Britishers. Post-independence in 1947 there were not many who were aware of this ancient heritage site. Sometime in the early 19th century, an inquisitive young person set out to discover the truth about the existence of Kanvashram. If not for him, the very presence of this ancient historical heritage site would never ever seen the light of the day, resulting in a nation not being aware of its creator. A visitor to this nation on learning of the few facts about Kanvashram stated, "If all this was in some other nation, what all must have happened there". Very true, so it is necessary to take a step forward to unravel the history of Kanvashram and present it to the people so that something also happen here.

CHAPTER 1
HISTORY

The history of Kanvashram is extremely old indeed. Kanvashram was a fully developed spiritual, cultural and educational centre that existed in this subcontinent. It cannot be compared with anything, as nothing of that nature existed anywhere else on this subcontinent or on planet Earth, at that time. Changes that led to the creation of this ancient heritage site on the banks of river Malini, are of such immense magnitude that they must have taken hundreds of years, as nothing really happens all at once in this vast universe. Everything is in a state of motion, each inching forward at its own pace. There are no pauses. Changes take place over time, which causes civilisations to form and disappear. The wise *rishis* living on the banks of river Malini in the Kanvashram region have scripted in the oldest and the first book of knowledge Rig Veda, that the universe is alive, in motion and unending, something that cannot be fathomed.

In the present times, it is most likely that many amongst us are unaware of either the location or of the vibrant bond that existed between the ancient heritage site Kanvashram or Kanv *ka Ashram*, and the nation Bharat Varsh. This knowledge, possibly as of today, may be limited to some scholars, historians or some amongst us interested in the ancient heritage of this nation. However, all of us, the citizens of this ancient nation know that our country is called Bharat Varsh. Why? Possibly this is also in our knowledge, that our nation derives its name Bharat Varsh from Emperor Bharat, who with his dynamic and vibrant leadership integrated this vast land mass into one nation, for the first time, and ruled it for many decades. Thousands of years have passed since the creation of this ancient nation and its golden historic past. River Malini still streams down gently and softly from the folds of Shivalik mountain range. Sadly though, its banks are devoid of the world-famous education and spiritual centre, an ideal university, where students toiled to acquire knowledge under the guidance of the chancellor of the university, knowledgeable *rishi* Kanv. The place was immensely popular with saints and sages who resided in the ashrams, immersed in deep meditation, for spiritual solace and enlightenment, to understand the ultimate truth of life. The ashram must have been spread over a vast area, adjacent to the banks of river Malini, to accommodate *gurus,* pupils and other residents. The ashram possibly was established at more than one location, which were in proximity. It is possible that Kanv was not a person but a title that was bestowed to the chancellor of this university. It is also equally likely that Kanv was a subtitle affixed to the name of one of the chancellors of the university, to give him a distinctive identity. This practice to add a subtitle to one's name is still prevalent in the region. However, it is certain that the chancellor, whose name was Kanv or who had a subtitle Kanv affixed to his name, was the person under whose guidance the place functioned and was identified as Kanvashram.

Saraswati-Sindhu civilisation, which flourished on this subcontinent was mainly spread along the banks of rivers Sarasvati and Drishadvati. However, some settlements have been found close to river Sindhu (Indus) also. The earliest excavated settlements Mohenjo-Daro and Harappa are close to river Sindhu. Excavation of settlements along the bank of river Sarasvati suggests that the sites found along its bank are older than the initial excavated sites like Mohenjo-Daro and Harappa. The Sarasvati-Sindhu civilisation has now been estimated to have originated about ~7500 BCE or earlier as per recent excavation. It was spread over a vast area in the states of Haryana, Punjab, Rajasthan, Gujrat, Jammu & Kashmir etc. in India. The civilisation developed and its matured period is estimated to be from ~2700 BCE. Then for some unknown reason the well settled civilisation began to disintegrate and its collapse commenced from ~2300 BCE and it ultimately came to a gradual end by ~1900 BCE. There are many reasons that caused its disintegration but the primary reason has been attributed to the drying up of the mighty river Sarasvati. All this happened thousands of years before the nation Bharat Varsh as a nation came into existence. The subcontinent as a nation came into being, during the reign of Emperor Bharat, around ~1600 BCE. The time of the reign of Emperor Bharat is determined based on the year of happening of the great war described in the epic Mahabharat, fought on the vast plains of Kurukshetra.

Many dates are assigned by different historians, about the period of the great war between Pandav and Kaurav. Some are based on astronomical data and others on various other methods of calculations but most are of the opinion that the war took place sometime around 1000 BCE. Archaeological Survey India (ASI) based on its analysis and research has concluded that the Mahabharat war took place between 1100 and 1200 BCE. With the datum point fixed the year of birth of Bharat, son of King Dushyant and Shakuntala, in Kanvashram can be inferred. Emperor Bharat was born 16 generations before Kaurav and Pandav, who were his direct descendants (**Figure 03**). Bhandarkar Institute of Oriental Studies, Pune, India established in 1926, has carried out a detailed study of different versions of Mahabharat available in this nation. Based on the study of the documents written in different languages they published a critical edition of Mahabharat in Sanskrit, which has now been translated into English. The family chart of the lineage of Emperor Bharat drawn up by them is identical to the chart printed by Gita

Lineage of Emperor Bharat

Bharat -m- Sunanda

Bhumanyu --m--- Vijaya

Suhotra – m - Suvarn

Hasti – m- Yasodra (Established Hastinapur)

Vikunthan – m – Sudeva

Anjamidh – m – Kaikeyi, Nagi, Gandhari, Vimla & Riksha

Savaram – m - Tapati

Kuru – m - Subhangi

Vidhurath – m - Sanpriya

Anshav – m - Amrita

Parikshit – m - Suyasa

Bhimsen – m - Kumari

Prartishiva – m -Sunanda

Satyavati-------m--------Shantanu--------m--------Ganga

-----------Amba & Ambalika--- m--Vichatravir   Devvrat (Bhishma)

Dvaipyana

Dhritarashtra – m -Ghandari   Pandu – m -Kunti

Duryodhan , Dushasan etc **(Kauravas)**

Yudhistar, Bhim, Arjun, Nakul, Shadev **(Pandavas)**

Fig 03. Lineage of Emperor Bharat

Press Gorakhpur, Uttar Pradesh, in the Mahabharat published by them in Hindi. Both have concluded that there is a difference of 16 generations between Pandav/Kaurav and Emperor Bharata. Taking a rough estimate of 30 year period of a generation, Emperor Bharat must have been born about ~500 years before the great war.

No physical remains of that period have been found along the banks of river Malini, in the region, which can be identified with the existence of Kanvashram. Also, there is no mention of Kanvashram in any history book of this nation. It is as if the place never existed. Besides no dedicated excavation work has been undertaken in the region by the Archaeological Survey of India (ASI) or any other independent institution, though at many locations, relics and other artifacts have been unearthed in the region currently since 1991. The earliest known relics have been found in the region as early as 1924. The remains of monuments and relics are being unearthed on a regular basis, due to soil erosion in a particular area in the Kanvashram region. Most of the artifacts of monuments have been dated to the 10th century or later by Garhwal University, Srinagar **(Appendix A)**. ASI, Circle Dehradun, Uttarakhand in its initial preliminary report submitted to ASI, HQ, New Delhi in Sep 2012, has also corroborated this fact in their report that the artifacts found date back to be between 9 to 11th century CE **(Appendix B)**. Despite lack of any physical or archaeological evidence on ground, presence of Kanvashram cannot be set aside. Documentary evidence available points to the fact that sometime in the past, an ashram of sage Kanv, existed on the banks of river Malini. Some ancient scriptures of the nation do hold sketchy references to the presence of Kanvashram. It is certain that in the near future when excavation is carried out in the region, enough physical evidence will be found, which will corroborate the physical existence of Kanvashram, and force the historians to rewrite the history of this nation.

Reference to the existence of Kanvashram exists in ancient documents like Puranas, Mahabharat and in the literary creation of eminent poet Kalidas. From a religious point of view also, Kanvashram was considered a prominent holy heritage site, that was equated and placed above other important holy sites of this nation, like Badri Dham (Badrinath) and Kedar Dham (Kadar Nath). The prominence of the place can be gauged by the fact that Kanvashram has been referred to in ancient scriptures and epics written in this nation. In one of the *Puranas*, the following couplet in Sanskrit enumerates the importance of the place,

ततः कण्वआश्रम गत्वा बद्रीनाथ क्षेत्र के ततः ।

तेपेसु सर्वेसु स्नानचैव यथा विधि।।

ततः केदार भवनम गच्छे पापनु पतये केदारनाथ ।

शस भमूजय गृहतयाज्ञा ततः सिद्ध कार्य बद्रीकेसय दर्शनम शुभदायक ।।

In the *shlok,* a message is addressed to complete humanity stating that *"before entering the pious Badrinath region or proceeding for pilgrimage to Badrinath, all pilgrims should come to Kanvashram. After undertaking the ritual bath, they should proceed to Kedar Nath and it is after that only they should visit Badrinath. In this way only will the pilgrimage be fruitful and work planned completed successfully."*

The ancient saying amply highlights the importance of Kanvashram as a religious site. In another reference in the 57th chapter of the *Skanda Purana,* the *shlok* highlights the brilliance and glorifies the power of the sage Kanv and Kanvashram,

कण्वआश्रम समारमभ यावननदं गिरि भवेत तावत
क्षेत्र परमं भुक्ति - मुक्ति परदायकः ।

कण्वोनाम महातेज महार्षि लोक विश्रुतः
तसया श्रम पदे भगवत रमापतिम् । ।

"Kanvashram which extends from here to the Nandgiri mountain, is an extremely holy place and a centre of spiritual devotion and enlightenment. For here is the ashram of the world-renowned and brilliant saint Kanv. Peace and tranquility can be achieved by paying tribute to the pious sage there."

However, the most prominent and detailed source of information about the existence of Kanvashram is Mahabharat. In the chapter *Sambhavparv* of Mahabharat, the ashram's presence on the bank of river Malini is described with all the events that happened therein. This includes detailed narration, from the birth of Emperor Bharat to events leading to his coronation as King. The information about Kanvashram is described in 418 *shloks* in the Mahabharat (Sanskrit – Hindi edition), printed by Gorakhpur Press. In the 69th chapter *shlok* 1, Janmejay, great grandson of Arjun, requests the *Sauti* (story teller) Vaishampayan,

सम्भव भरतस्याहं चरितं च महामते ।

सकुन्तलायाश्चोतेपत्तिं श्रोतुमिच्छामि तत्त्वत।।

Brahman! I would like to know about the birth and character of the extremely intelligent Bharat and the events about the birth of Shakuntala, all in actual detail.

In reply to this question, Vaishampayan proceeds to narrate the sacred stories of Mahabharat, composed by Krishn Dwaipayan, which were heard by him. Before describing about the birth and life of Emperor Bharat, the storyteller instead commences his narrative with a description of King Dushyant. He tells the assembled people that once upon a time, there was a gallant and brave king Dushyant, who was loved and respected by his subjects. He further goes on to describe his kingdom as a place where all people lived happily, without fear and were well protected by the king. The storyteller thereafter narrates about a hunting trip undertaken by the king accompanied by his army in the dense forest located to the East of his kingdom. King Dushyant, while chasing a deer, emerges from the dense forest into an open area where Kanvashram is located. Though most agree that the king left his capital for hunting, how or why he reached the ashram differs in documents, which describe the event. At this juncture, the question that surfaces is, was King Dushyant aware of the ashram and went there to meet sage Kanv or did he become aware of the presence of the ashram and came there to investigate or did he stumble upon the ashram by chance while on the hunt? All these questions have different answers. Was this the first interaction between the two communities? The answers to some of these questions will be addressed later in succeeding chapters. For the present, we will continue our quest to find historical evidence about the existence of Kanvashram.

In *Sambhvparv,* Chapter 70, *shlok* 21. Mahabharat (Geeta Press, Gorakhpur) describes that on reaching the shores of the river Malini and on seeing the ashram, the same is described by the king,

महाकच्छैर्बृहद्भिश्च विभ्राजितमतीय च।

मालिनीमभितो राजन नदीं पुण्यां सुखोदकाम।।

The ashram is located on both banks of the holy river Malini whose water is tasty and sweet. The tall trees present in and around the ashram have added to its beauty and grandeur. In yet another *shlok* in *Sambhavparv*,

प्रस्थे हिमवतो रम्ये मालिनीममितो नदीम् ।
जातमुत्सृज्यन्तं गर्भं मेनका मलिनिमनुः । ।

Located at the extreme end of the snow-covered mountains is a region, on the bank of river Malini, where Shakuntala, born out of the womb of Menka, has given birth to a child. In the *shlok* the child referred to is Bharat, who is born to Shakuntala, who is the daughter of Menka. The narrative in Mahabharat thereafter continues with King Dushyant meeting Shakuntala, marrying her and the birth of their son Bharat. In the last but one *shlok* covering the complete narrative about the birth of Bharat in Kanvashram and his coronation as a king in Mahabharat, *Sambharvaparva* chapter 72 *shlok* 131, the following is written:

भरताद् भारती कीर्तिर्येनेदं भारतं कुलम।
अपरे ये च पूर्वे वै भारता इति विश्रुता:।।

This land mass has been named Bharat after Emperor Bharat. All the great and mighty kings born in this family after him who became famous have been called descendants of Bharat.

From all the details enumerated in the epic Mahabharat, it is amply clear that sage Kanv lived in an ashram called Kanvashram, which was located on the banks of river Malini. It was here Shakuntala gave birth to a child, who later went on to become Emperor Bharat, after whose name this nation is called Bharat Varsh and generations thereafter were identified with him. Though the complete historical details about the birth of Bharat and his coronation have been described in Mahabharat in explicit detail, the time frame as to when all these events occurred, is not specified anywhere.

However, the person who brought forth the fading memory of the existence of Kanvashram once again into public domain, about a millennium after the great war was poet, writer and dramatist Kalidas. There are different views about the period in which he lived. Some place him with the legendary king Vikramaditya of Ujjain who ruled sometime around 57 BCE. Other historians are of the opinion that he flourished during the reign of Chandragupta II, (380–415 CE) who was also called Vikramaditya, and ruled from Ujjain and Kalidas was one of the nine gems of courtiers in his court. The period Kalidas lived is not really under consideration here. What is an undebatable historical fact is that Kalidas was the person who authored a number of classical literary works, which are recognized as his authentic creations, by one and all. The issue that is of interest at this juncture is where Kalidas was born and where he spent his childhood and adulthood. The complete narrative of events and happenings in Kanvashram has been woven into a drama and presented in the form of a literary work by Kalidas. The complete world is indebted to him for this extraordinary creation. Though the ferocity of time has destroyed every trace of the physical existence of Kanvashram, Kalidas made

Kanvashram and all those associated with it, immortal in his world-famous creation Abhigyan Shakuntalam. With his picturesque and charming language, he made Kanvashram come alive once again thousands of years afterward. The vibrant description of Kanvashram, on the bank of river Malini, scripted in the drama, is mesmerizing and captivating. The drama revolves around Shakuntala, daughter of Menka-Vishvamitra who was brought up by *rishi* Kanv in his ashram, her *gandharv* marriage to King Dushyant and the birth of their son Bharat. One aspect which can be concluded from the detailed description of Kanvashram in Abhigyan Shakuntalam, is that Kalidas must have lived close to Kanvashramn. In his other creation Meghdoot, Kalidas has described a region that synchronizes with the topography of the state of Uttarakhand where Kanvashram is located. It therefore seems certain that Kalidas had travelled in and around the Kanvashram region extensively in his early years. This gives support to the opinion expressed by the people of Uttarakhand, that Kalidas was born in Uttarakhand. As per local legend in Uttarakhand, the place of birth of Kalidas has been accepted as Kabhilta, District -Rudraprayag, Uttarakhand. Annual fair is held every year in Kabhilta to honour and celebrate his birth. Kabhilta is not very distant from river Malini, where Kanvashram is located.

In the first chapter of his world-famous drama Abhigyan Shakuntalam, the poet describes the scene where King Dushyant out on a hunt reaches the shores of river Malini.

He comes across some sage collecting wood from the river bank of a river. When asked, who they are, they tell the King *"The ashram of our Guru, Chancellor Kanv rishi, can be seen at a distance on the bank of the river Malini."*

एष खलु कण्वस्य कुलपते रनुमालिनीतीरे अश्रमो दृश्यते ।।
अभिज्ञान शाकुन्तलम प्रथम अंक

In this verse, Kalidas addresses sage Kanv as कुलपते, translated as Chancellor of a university. Addressing sage Kanv as chancellor, clearly implies that Kanvashram was in fact a university or an educational centre and *rishi* Kanv was the Chancellor. In four different places in the drama, the writer has addressed sage Kanv as Chancellor. The concept of the ashram is not as accepted or understood in the present day. In today's understanding, an ashram is a place where one can rest and stay overnight while on a visit to a religious site. During the Vedic period, an ashram was a place where people lived in-house to acquire knowledge under the guidance of a sage or a *guru*. In this form of educational system children at a very young age came to live in the ashram, to acquire knowledge under the guidance and directions of a *Guru,* for a fixed period. Institutes that came up later under this education system, came to be addressed as *Gukukul.*

In chapter 5 of the drama Abhigyan Shakuntalam a messenger informs King Dushyant "*Victory to the King! There are some people who have come to meet you who positively appear to be from the snow-covered mountain region and have brought a message for you from sage Kanv. There are some women with them."*

जयति जयति देवः।
एतेखलु हिमगिरेरूपत्यकारम्यवासिनःकण्वसंदेस
मादाय सस्त्रीकाः तपस्विनः सम्प्राप्ताः।। अभि0 शा0 पंच्म अंक

In the 7th chapter of Abhigyan Shakuntalam, the sage Kanv blesses the child and says that *this child riding on his strong chariot will win over the earth, made up of seven islands or regions and no one will be able to challenge him. As he has been harassing all the animals in this ashram, he was named Sarvadaman (one who dominates), but in the future as he will be responsible for taking care of the complete world and providing for all the living beings in it, he will be called Bharat.*

रथेनायुध्द तस्तिमितगतिना तीर्णजलधि,
पुरा सप्तव्दीपां जयति वसुगामप्रतिरथ ।।

इहांय सत्त्वानां प्रसभदमनात्सर्वमन ।
पुनर्यास्यत्याख्यां भरत इति लोकस्य भरणात्।।

The drama endorses the fact that the ashram of sage Kanv was on the bank of river Malini, where Bharat was born. The drama corroborates the facts about the presence of Kanvashram enumerated in the epic Mahabharat.

Greek historian and explorer Magesthanese visited the court of Chandra Gupta Maurya, reigning king of this nation. He stayed in his court, in the capital Patliputra for five years (302 -298 BC). He travelled throughout his vast kingdom. Based on his observations and experiences he wrote a book called Indica. Though the book is not in existence anymore, those who read the book have written about its contents. The book possibly was either destroyed or forcibly put out of circulation, at a later date. The reason is that Magesthanese in his book has idealized Indian culture and praised it in no uncertain terms. This was not acceptable to the Greeks and subsequently to the Western historians. Those who had read the book recalled the fragmented details, consolidated the bits and reproduced the same in different books published by them, which are still available. In the book Indica, Megatheres referred to a river Eeriness. He writes that Kanvashram was situated on the bank of river Malini, where Shakuntala grew up. This fact has also been confirmed by Alexander Cunningham, Chief of the Archaeological Department in India during the British occupation of this nation, that the river Eeriness mentioned by Megatheres is none other than river Malini.

An administration system of assimilation of information in the form of printed documents was introduced by the colonial rulers in this nation which provided information about individual districts and states. These documents, published on a regular basis, were called a Gazette. The Gazette published contained geographical, climatic and social conditions prevalent in the region. It was regularly updated with fresh information and republished. The publication of Gazettes possibly commenced sometime in the early 20th

century or maybe earlier. Post-independence also, the gazette continued to be published by the Government of India and respective states. The gazette published for District Pauri Garhwal by the Government of Uttar Pradesh in 1967 (a photocopy of the gazette was obtained by the writer from the archive of the Uttar Pradesh state government, Lucknow) besides other information, gives a brief description of various rivers flowing in the district. This geographical information was possibly endorsed in the gazette when it was printed for the first time. In respect of the river Malini the gazette, besides specifying its geographical location, also clearly highlights the historical importance of the river. **(Figure 04)**

"It is a river is of some historical interest. It has been tentatively identified with the Eeriness mentioned about 300 BC by the Greek ambassadors Magesthanese; some 250 years later the poet Kalidas immortalized the stream in his famous drama Abhigyan Shakuntalam. It was on the banks of the Malini that king Dushyant, pursued an antelope to its refuge in the shrine of the rishi Kanv and it was in the forest on the river bank Dushyant first met Shakuntala, his future queen. Canals have been taken out from the river just below the Chawkighat to irrigate the area in the bhabar."

Although, undoubtedly Mahabharat is the oldest source of information about Kanvashram, there were many, who with their untiring efforts kept the memories of Kanvashram alive through their writing. Though there exists a gap of downe near the Gaula where it receives the Mandal. It then flows through the tahsil in an easterly direction as far as its junction with the Palain, about 3 km. north of the Baksar rest house. Turning south-ward and flowing for some kilometres through tahsil Lansdowne, it leaves the district near Kalagarh. The river always contains water and during the rains is a seething torrent, debouching on the plains at Kalagarh.

Malin—The river, a tributary of the Ganga, bears this name when it issues from the hills at Chaukighat. In the upper reaches it is known as the Saurgadh, its source being among the ranges to the east of the Saur village in *patti* Walla Ajmer. It first runs in a westerly direction as far as the village of Ranesa, then takes a southerly direction till it leaves the district near the village of Haldu Khata. It is a river of some historical interest. It has been tentatively identified with the Erineses mentioned about 300 B. C. by the Greek ambassador, Megasthenes ; some 250 years later the poet Kalidasa immortalized the stream in his famous drama, *Abhigyan Shakuntalam*. It was on the banks of the Malin that the king Dushyanta, persued an antelope to its refuge in the shrine of the rishi Kanva and it was in the forest on the river bank Dushyanta first met Shakuntala, his future queen. Canals have been taken out from the river just below the Chaukighat to irrigate the areas in the *bhabar*.

Mandal—This river, a tributary of the Ramganga, rises on the southern slope of the ranges lying in the eastern parts of *pattis* Talla Badalpur and Painon of pargana Talla Salan and has three main sources. The most westerly, rising near Maraura in Talla Badalpur, takes a south-south-easterly course through Painon and passing the village of Jamri and Dabrya joins, near Jhart, the main branch which rises close by in the eastern declivities of the Dhargaon range. The third branch drains the eastern part of *patti* Painon and flowing nearly due south by Badiyargaon and Kotri joins the main stream at Raunderi. The united stream

Fig 04a UP District Gazetteers- Garwhal

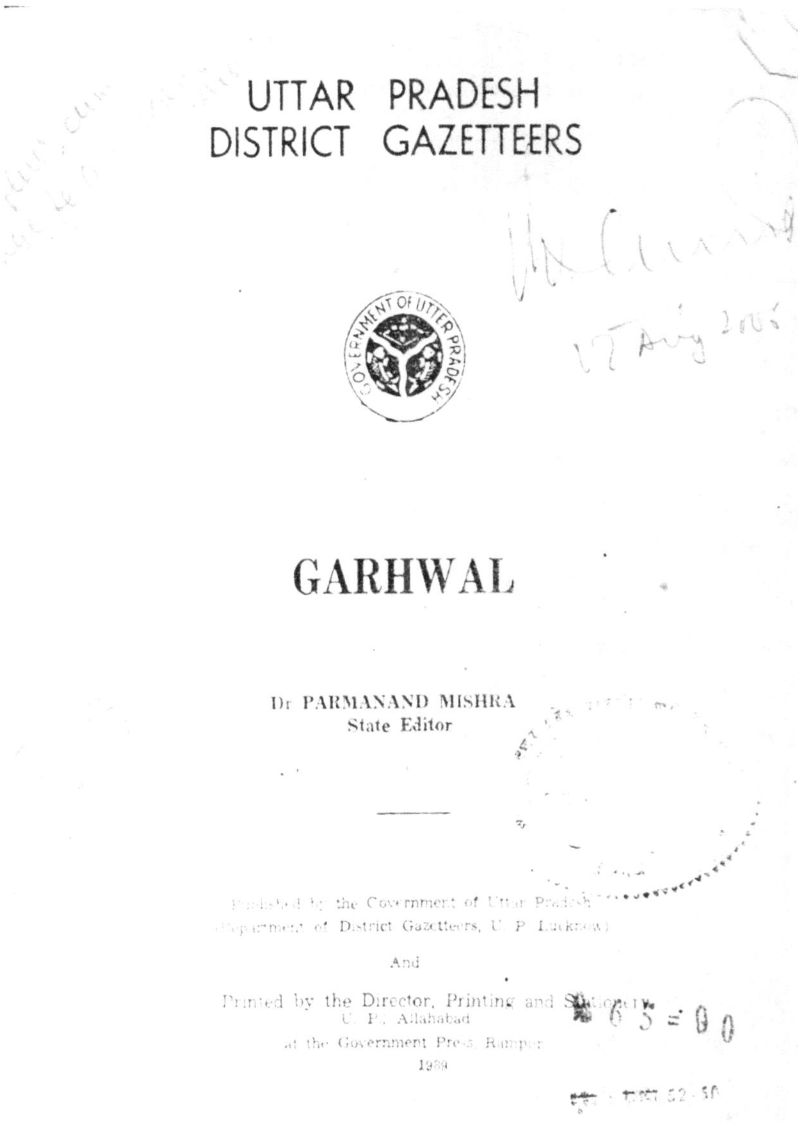

UTTAR PRADESH
DISTRICT GAZETTEERS

GARHWAL

Dr PARMANAND MISHRA
State Editor

Published by the Government of Uttar Pradesh
(Department of District Gazetteers, U. P. Lucknow)

And

Printed by the Director, Printing and Stationery
U. P., Allahabad
at the Government Press, Rampur
1989

Fig 04b UP District Gazetteers- Garwhal

thousands of years between the presentation of Abhigyan Shakuntalam by Kalidas to the world and the next author writing about the existence of the heritage site Kanvashram. It was in the early 20th century that a person took up the task of highlighting the existence of Kanvashram. It is possible that many others may have written about the famous heritage site. Somehow, no documented information about their efforts is available. All those who have written about Kanvashram are collectively responsible for keeping the memory of the famous Vedic educational centre alive and resonating in the memory of the people of this nation. The person who was at the forefront to revive the lost identity of Kanvashram was Srinidhi Sidhantalankar, an explorer and a writer. Based on information made available in his books, a memorial was erected on the left bank of river Malini, opposite the hamlet Chawkighat in 1956 by the Uttar Pradesh government. Details about his contribution to Kanvashram are enumerated in the succeeding chapter.

The evidence available is irrefutable and proves that the ancient heritage site, Kanvashram was located on the banks of river Malini. It also confirms that the creator of this nation, Emperor Bharat was born and brought up in this ashram. Still, there are several dots that need to be connected, to fill the canvas and get a complete picture of the heritage site. The primary question is where was Kanvashram physically located on the ground? How large an area was it spread on? River Malini flows from its origin for 80 km, before it merges into river Ganga, somewhere along its long undulating path, the heritage site was located. Finally, if all the above questions are resolved satisfactorily the ultimate question that needs an answer is, why did the ancestors of sage Kanv choose river Malini, discarding all other major rivers flowing in the region? What factors influenced the decision to establish the ashram on the banks of Malini? Lastly, who were these people? Where had they come from? Maybe, all the questions may not be answered conclusively in the succeeding chapters by me but still effort needs to be made in that direction.

CHAPTER 2

WHERE WAS KANVASHRAM PHYSICALLY LOCATED?

With all the evidence presented in the preceding chapter it can be inferred that Kanvashram was located on the banks of river Malini. However, it is difficult to deduce the actual physical location of Kanvashram on ground, based on the information available in various ancient scriptures. Some geographical and topographical details are available but these are sketchy and do not point to a specific location. A fact that has been repeated time and again, is the proximity of the ashram close to river Malini. Both Mahabharata and Abhigyan Shakuntalam, have specifically referred to river Malini and related the river with Kanvashram, though there is a large time gap between the scripting of the two documents. Abhigyan Shakuntalam was written by Kalidas in the 1st century. Mahabharat is an offshoot of the book Bharat, created by adding about ~70,000 verses to it. Book Bharat was created from the original epic called Jaya by addition of ~10,000 verses. There are different opinions about the time and number of verses added and how the original book Jaya was transformed into Bharat and later into Mahabharat. At what stage of transformation, the story of King Dushyant and Shakuntala was added to the epic, cannot be stated with certainty but as it appears in the initial chapters of the epic, it must have formed part of the original book Jaya. The addition to the original book Jaya and its ultimate transformation into Mahabharat must have taken place over a fairly long period of time. The original epic Jaya (meaning "victory" in Hindi) could have been scripted possibly around ~500 BCE. This is an assumption and I do not have any concrete evidence about the time of scripting of Jaya. However, some happenings in that period point in that direction. If we proceed further based on the geographical and historical data available, we observe that there is only one river Malini which exists in this subcontinent and it flows in the state of Uttarakhand, originating from the folds of the Shivalik mountain ranges at Chandakhal next to a village Malya or Maliniya. The river spouts from the base of a hill. It exits from the mountainous region into the plain terrain at Chawkighat, a hamlet which lies about 12 km East of town Kotdwara, District- Pauri Garhwal, Uttarakhand. **(Figure 14)** River Malini thereafter traverses through the plain region before finally flowing into the mighty river Ganga at Ravali, Uttar Pradesh**. (Figure 16)**

As of date no physical search for the presence of Kanvashram has been undertaken by the government of India or any other agency, along the river. A reasonable study of the path of the river Malini done by me from its origin to Chawkighat has not revealed any physical evidence, in the form of archaeological remains, indicating the presence of some ancient settlement. Neither has any explorer or writer indicated the presence of any archaeological remains in the Malini valley, or along its path in the hilly section. Archaeological remains have been found around Chawkighat, in the recent past but these have been dated to between 1000 to 1200 CE. No local tales or folk songs are in circulation, which connect Kanvashram to a particular place, are recited by the local people in the region. Some locations along the river Malini, have names that are identified with some personalities associated with Kanvashram. A ridge of a hill range, along the river Malini is referred to as *Sountiyal Dhar*, identifying the place with Shakuntala. **(Figure 05)** *Dhar* is a word in local Garhwali language, to describe a lowest point in a ridge in a mountain range. Such a depression in a range is called a 'Saddle'. Vistar Katil, is another location that lies close to *Sauntiyal Dhar and is* associated with *rishi* Vishwamitra. Menka, mother of Shakuntala, is associated with Menka *Shila.* A rock lying close to caves on the hillside in the Malini valley. The complete region including Chawkighat till 2018 was called Kalalghati. In the older official records, the area was referred to as Kolughati. In some other documents, the region was called Karalghati. These names Kalalghati, Kolughati, Karalghati etc. have evolved from their original name Kanvghati, which indicates the presence of Kanvashram. Taking this fact into account the present government of Uttarakhand, India, has issued a gazette and renamed the region as Kanvghati. **(Figure 06)**

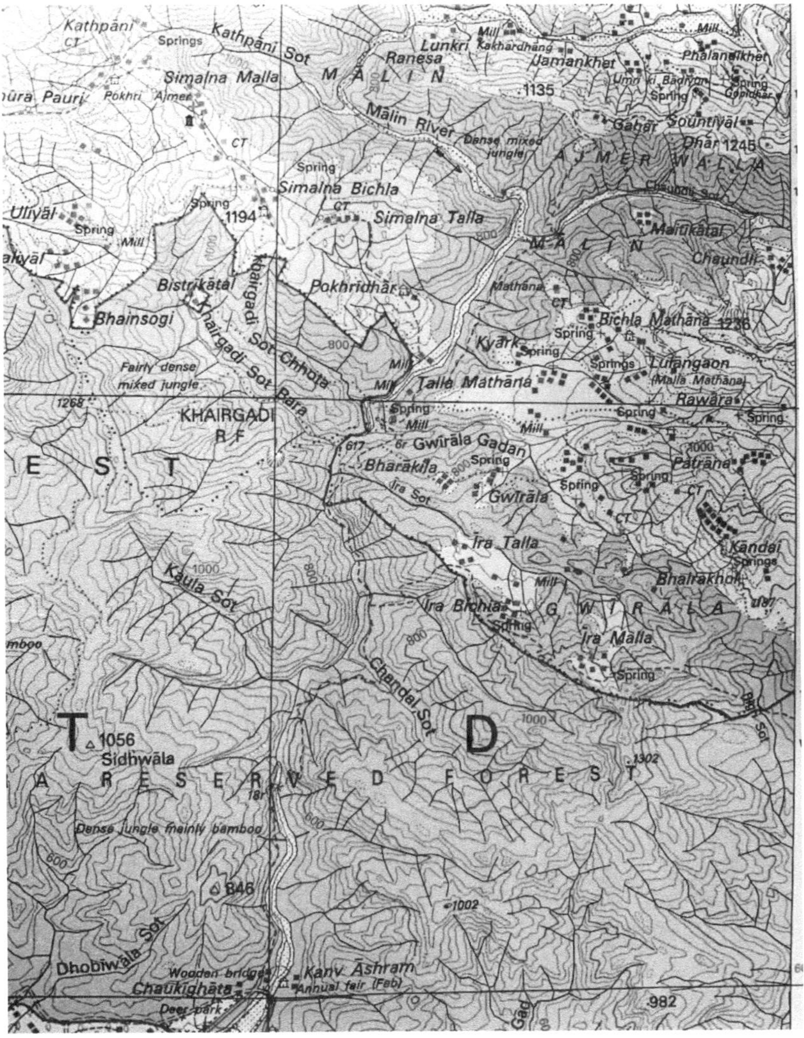

Fig 05 Sountiyal Dhar marked in Survey of India Map

उत्तराखण्ड शासन
शहरी विकास अनुभाग–2
संख्या– 1352/IV(2)-श0वि0–2020–08(मु0म0पौ0)/20
देहरादून: दिनांक 16, दिसम्बर, 2020

विज्ञप्ति

एतद्द्वारा उत्तर प्रदेश पुनर्गठन अधिनियम 2000 की धारा 06 के अन्तर्गत जनपद पौड़ी गढ़वाल कोटद्वार क्षेत्र के 'कलालघाटी' का नाम परिवर्तित करते हुए कण्वघाटी किया जाता है।

यह आदेश तत्काल प्रभाव से लागू होगा।

(शैलेश बगौली)
सचिव।

संख्या– 1352/IV(2)-श0वि0–2020–08(मु0म0पौ0)/2020 तद्दिनांकित।
प्रतिलिपि निम्नलिखित को सूचनार्थ एवं आवश्यक कार्यवाही हेतु प्रेषित –

1. मुख्य सचिव, निजी सचिव, उत्तराखण्ड शासन।
2. समस्त अपर मुख्य सचिव/प्रमुख सचिव/सचिव/प्रभारी सचिव, उत्तराखण्ड शासन।
3. आयुक्त, कुमाँऊ मण्डल/गढ़वाल मण्डल, उत्तराखण्ड।
4. निदेशक, शहरी विकास विभाग, उत्तराखण्ड देहरादून।
5. समस्त जिलाधिकारी, उत्तराखण्ड।
6. समस्त नगर आयुक्त, अधिशासी अधिकारी, नगर निगम/नगर पालिका परिषद/नगर पंचायत, उत्तराखण्ड। (द्वारा निदेशक, शहरी विकास निदेशालय, देहरादून)
7. गार्ड फाईल।

आज्ञा से,

(शैलेश बगौली)
सचिव।

Fig 06 Gazette Kalalghati to Kanvghati

Though bits and pieces of information are available about Kanvashram, all this cannot be termed as complete and thorough. Systematic search and archaeological excavation in the region needs to be carried out, to uncover the facts. Kanvashram did exist around ~1600 BCE. Where exactly was Kanvashram geographically or physically located on the 80 km long undulating path of river Malini? On which bank of the river was it located? The epic Mahabharat links up some of the physical elements and people associated with Kanvashram but does not reveal the true physical location of Kanvashram. Two aspects of the ashram are not revealed in the epic. Firstly, the period of existence of Kanvashram and secondly the exact physical location on ground of the ashram. References about Kanvashram are also given in *Puranas* but do not provide answers to these two primary questions. To get an answer about the location of the ashram, it is necessary to turn to Abhigyan Shakuntalam.

Kanvashram could have been located in any of the five distinct regions along the path of river Malini, whose 20 km stretch lies in the mountainous region, between Chawkighat and Chandakhal, place of origin or in the 60 km flow path of the river in the plain region, which stretches from Chawkighat to Ravali. Firstly, Kanvashram could have been located somewhere in the plain region. The second possibility is that the ashram was located at Ravali, the place where Malini merges into river Ganga. The third possible location could be that it was in the mountainous region. The location of the ashram at the source of the river, in Malini valley should also be considered. Lastly, the location of the ashram at the point where the river exits from the mountain into the plain region at Chawkighat needs to be explored.

The longest stretch of the river Malini is in the plain region. With the changing weather pattern over the centuries, the quantum of flow in most of the rivers flowing in the subcontinent has considerably reduced. Hence, like all other rivers, river Malini also now carries less water in its bed, post-monsoon season. Reduction in flow can be attributed to the gradual warming of the planet which has taken place in the last ~150 years. Reduced flow of water in the summer season from April to June, has been observed by me in the last 30 years of my stay in the region. A portion of river water is tapped about a kilometre upstream of Chawkighat and fed into an irrigation canal, constructed prior to 1947. The network of canals was expanded in 1972, to irrigate the increased land under cultivation in the region. However, during the three months of monsoon season, July to September, the cascade of water that flows down the Malini valley is extremely heavy. The river overflows its banks and floods the plain, as its bed in this region is shallow, due gradual deposition of sand and gravel. With yearly flooding, the possibility of establishing an ashram anywhere along its bank in the plain region or at the place where Malini merges into the Ganga, does not seem to be a practical option. Besides, King Dushyant had travelled a considerable distance, while on a hunt, through the forest before he encountered a slight upward gradient in the terrain, which indicates that he had reached close to the mountainous region. However, there are some, unable to visualize the period when the flow of the river Malini and river Ganga must have been extremely heavy, to claim that Kanvashram was located at Ravali. Claims have also been made of the existence of Kanvashram, in different parts of this nation, without any authentic facts or figures to support their claim.

The next place up for consideration, is Malini valley itself, including the place of origin of the river. The river valley is quite enormous and has a catchment area of about ~75,000 hectares. In the past the valley must have been inaccessible, being surrounded by high mountain range and dense forest, though it may have been possible to reach the valley by travelling along the river in the summer months. Even today, it is extremely difficult to track along the river, due to the presence of huge boulders and the necessity to criss-cross the river, at numerous points, to move forward. Legend is that the ashram of sage Vishvamitra was close to the Malini valley, where he resided, engrossed in deep meditation, to enhance his spiritual capabilities. Disturbed by his deep penance and meditation, Lord Indra sends fairy Menka from heaven to distract him. With her beauty and charm, Menka succeeded in doing so. A girl child was born out of their union. Having achieved her objective, Menka left the girl child in the jungle and returned to heaven. The child was found by sage Kanv and brought up by him in his ashram and was named Shakuntala. The actual happenings may be somewhat different from the events narrated in different scriptures. Vishvamitra must have been residing in his ashram with his wife. Menka, wife of Vishvamitra, may have died (departed for heaven) while giving birth to the child or shortly afterwards. Not able to manage the newborn child, Vishvamitra handed over the child to sage Kanv, who had female residents in his ashram. Shakuntala thereafter was brought up in Kanvashram. According to one legend Shakuntala and her son did not go back to Kanvashram after being turned away by King Dushyant but on return resided in *Sountiyal Dhar,* a place close to the ashram of her biological father *rishi* Vishvamitra. It was here she brought up her son Bharat. Malini valley is associated with sage Vishvamitra and Shakuntala and there is no other legend present which indicates the presence of Kanvashram in the valley. Further as narrated in Abhigyan Shakuntalam, king Dushyant is described as having reached close to the ashram on his chariot and after dismounting, walked some distance on foot to reach the ashram. The path of the river in the mountainous section is treacherous and full of natural obstacles. No chariot can traverse this undulating terrain. Walking to the valley through the dense forest seems a difficult task to be undertaken by a king. Hence the possibility of the Kanvashram being in the valley can be ruled out.

So that leaves us with one final option. The place where the river Malini exits the mountain into the plain region at Chawkighat. The presence of ashram at this location should not be taken for granted. The place needs to be explored for physical telltale signs of the presence of ashram on the ground and confirmation done based on information available in documents. The first indication of the ashram location is provided in Abhigyan Shakuntalam by poet Kalidas. The hunting episode of King Dushyant and his entry into the ashram is described in the first chapter of Abhigyan Shakuntalam. Though, Kalidas has inserted an emotional angle to the event and scripted it in a different manner, to what is written in Mahabharat. Kalidas describes that King Dushyant whilst chasing a deer, reaches close to the ashram. The person steering the chariot, addresses Dushyant and says "O King! I have to pull the reins of the chariot, to reduce its speed, as we are now traversing on uneven and sloping land". Implying that they had left the plain terrain and were now moving on a terrain with a slight upwards gradient.

उघ्दातिनी भूमिरितिणयीषशिमसयमनाद्रखस्य मंदीकृती वेगः।

At this juncture, as it became difficult to steer the chariot, Dushyant dismounted and walked to the river Malini flowing close by. It is here he encounters some sage collecting woods on the bank of the river. The king inquires as to who they are and what they are doing there. The sage inform the king that they live in the ashram of *rishi* Kanv.

When asked about the ashram, they point out to king Dushyant and say that "*the ashram of the chancellor Kanv can be seen at a distance upstream on the bank of river Malini.*

एष खलु कण्वस्य कुलपते रनुमालिनीतीरे अश्रमो दृश्यते ।।
अभिज्ञान शाकुन्तलम प्रथम अंक

To be able to see the ashram from a point downstream of the river, it had to be located at a slightly higher elevation. This implies that the ashram was situated on an elevated piece of land, next to the bank of river Malini and close to the place where King Dushyant had dismounted from his chariot. The location of the ashram further upstream can be ruled out, for it would not have been visible, as the river takes a turn at Chawkighat and thereafter moves in a zig-zag manner into the mountainous region. The ashram therefore was in the line of sight from where the king and the sages were standing. This is a crucial fact that fixes the location of the ashram. Further narration in Abhigyan Shakuntalam does not give away, as to on which bank of the river the ashram was located.

Mahabharat also provides some clues about the location of Kanvashram. The story of King Dushyant and all events connected with the birth of Bharat and his succession as king is enumerated in Mahabharat. Within the numerous stories written, the episode of king Dushyant's royal hunt is also described. As per Mahabharat, king Dushyant with his entourage crosses many dense forests during the hunt and enters an extremely enchanting forest full of flowering and fruit-laden trees. A *shlok* in Mahabharat besides describing the beauty of the ashram, reveals that the ashram was located on both banks of river Malini. The couplet describes the instant king Dushyant enters the ashram area– *That whilst engrossed in appreciating the beauty of the forest he (Dushyant) sights an ashram there. The ashram is located on both sides of the river Malini. The presence of huge trees around the ashram has added beauty to the ashram and the water of the river Malini flowing in between is sweet and pleasant.*

महाकच्छैर्बृहभ्दिशच विरभाजितमतीव च ।

मालिनीमभितो राजन् नदीं पुण्यां सुखोदकाम् ।।

Sambhavparv, Chapter 70, Mahabharat.

The ashram must have been in proximity to where king Dushyant dismounted from his chariot. As described, he stopped his entourage short of the ashram,

मुनीं विरजसं द्रष्टु गमिष्यामी तपोधनम्।

काशयपं स्थीयतामत्र यावदागमनं मम।।

Sambhavparv, Chapter 70, Mahabharat.

Addressing his army chiefs and soldiers he tells them that he is going to the ashram to meet Kashyap gotra rishi Kanv and instructs them to wait outside the ashram till his return.

Taking the above two narrations of the same episode described in Mahabharat and Abhigyan Shakuntalam and merging them together, gives us a clearer picture of the location of the ashram. Firstly, the presence of ashram on the bank of river Malini is endorsed. The second fact that emerges is that the ashram was located on both banks of the river Malini. Thirdly, the ashram was situated on elevated pieces of land next to the river bank. Do such elevated pieces of flat terrain suitable for ashram on both banks of the river still exist? For this, the terrain around the place where the river Malini exits the mountainous region needs to be examined. As of today, a small hamlet still exists at that spot, called Chawkighat. The name Chawkighat has been derived from two words, *Chowki* and *Gha*t. *Chowki* in Hindi, means a post or an outpost. The place was possibly a military outpost established at the boundary of his kingdom by the King of Garhwal, in 16th or 17th century CE, whose capital was in Srinagar, located deep in the hills, on the bank of river Ganga. The outpost must have served as a lookout for the encroaching enemy from the plain region towards the kingdom. The word, *Ghat* is a place where the dead are cremated by Hindus *sanatan dharma* rituals. Besides cremation of the dead, a *ghat* is also associated with religious rituals, which are performed by pilgrims, by taking a holy bath in a river. After taking a bath in the river Malini, pilgrims continued their pilgrimage to other holy sites in the Himalayas.

With its large in-house population of students, *gurus* and their families living there, the ashram must have been spread over a large area and possibly in more than one location. A brief survey of the region around the exit point of the river, reveals flat plots located close to the river. These different locations must have made up the main ashram and its extension. All these locations are within a distance of ~1 km from each other. Further upstream the river flows through a narrow bed with steep banks. One kilometre upstream from Chawkighat, on the right bank of the river lies a flat area of about ~1 hectare. Due to the flat terrain, the place was selected by the Irrigation Department, Uttar Pradesh in 1972 to construct an irrigation system. The river water was tapped from that point and fed into the irrigation canal. No earth mover or mechanical machines were available then, which could have levelled the area, nor can any reach there even now. Pumps were installed to pump the river water for drinking purposes. Living quarters, generators, store rooms etc. were constructed. All the machinery and other equipment was transported manually. With no habitation around or upstream, the water at that point is uncontaminated, crystal clear and fit for drinking and cooking. However, this location was not the main ashram but an extension of the ashram. Traces of human habitation have been found in the area, in the form of relics and were observed by Srinidhi Sidhantalankar during his track along the river Malini, in the year 1943 and this has been mentioned by him in his

Fig 07 Relics Located near Pump house by me in 2014

book. The observations were made before the construction of the irrigation system, constructed to divert river water for irrigation. He also found relics of some ancient monuments lying around while exploring that area. A single piece of relic was spotted by me in the area in 2014 close to the same location. **(Figure 07)** Though these artifacts are of much later date, their presence points to the fact about continuity of human habitation in that region. Most of the signs or traces of human settlements on the surface in the area have now disappeared, due to increased human activity in the region.

Lying about half a kilometre upstream from Chawkighat on the left bank of the river Malini is another location which also must have been an extension of the main ashram. This location is also a flat terrain of about one hectare. Presently this place is locally known as *Satti Mathh* **(सती मठ).** How and when this place was so named is not known. *Mathh* is defined as a Buddhist religious centre. There is a strong possibility that a *Mathh* was possibly established in the location during the spread of Buddhism in this nation. About 5 kms downstream from this position lie the ruins of a well-established Buddhist centre, Mordwaj adjacent to a village Mathurapur Mor. **(Figure 01)** Some people still reside in *Satti Mathh*, though till 1990 their number was substantially high. The third site is located slightly away from the river in the jungle. It is about 1 km from *Satti Mathh*. This place is also a plain area of about one hectare and must have been part of Kanvashram and inhabited in the past. The site has many rocks, with depressions carved out in them. The hollow depression created could possibly be used for grinding food materials or for some religious rituals and is an indication of habitation. Similar rocks with depressions carved out in them are also present on top of the hillock lying, directly opposite *Satti Math,* on the other bank, and is called Raj Darbar by local inhabitants. **(Figure 08**) All the above three sites were possibly extensions of the main ashram. The main ashram was located on the elevated land, which lies on the right bank of the river, where the river Malini exits the mountainous region at Chawkighat. **(Figure 09)**

Fig 08 Photograph of the rock with depression in Raj Darbar

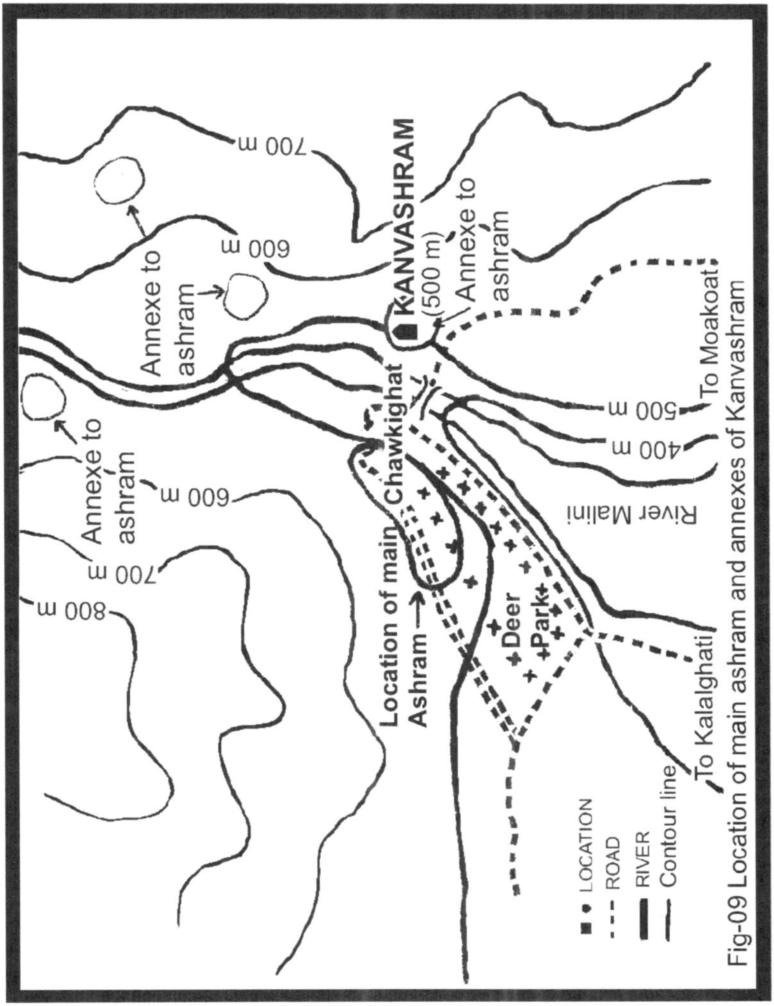

Fig-09 Location of main ashram and annexes of Kanvashram

The span of the river at this point is narrow. The river has a very heavy flow in the monsoon season but has not been able to erode the river banks at this point, due presence of a large natural rock formation, about ~200 meter long, along the right bank of the river. Most of the other extensions of the ashram located adjacent to the bank of the river have also not been encroached upon by the river as they are also on slightly elevated land from the river bed. By walking away and upwards from the river bank, on a 45-degree gradient, one reaches a flat stretch of land, at a height of about 50 to 60 mts. Overlooking from this location, one can view a long stretch of river Malini flowing below. Its proximity to the river, lying on an elevated piece of land and naturally protected from erosion by natural rock structure, makes the place an ideal location for the establishment of an ashram. The area of this flat piece of land is about ~15 hectares, sufficient to house a large population. **Figure 10 depicts the sketch of Kanvashram around 1600 BCE. Figure 11 is the drone shot of Kanvashram as it appears now.** Further, the land South of this plot is a gradual sloping terrain, which extends to as far as the eye can see. A forest guard outpost a forest rest house for the officials visiting the area was constructed on this plot during colonial rule. The forest rest house was later converted into a Tourist Guest House, by constructing new buildings by the Uttar Pradesh government. In 2023 it was refurbished and some new cottages were added. The guest house is operated by Garhwal Mandal Vikas Nigam,

Fig 10 A sketch of Kanvashram then around 1600 BCE

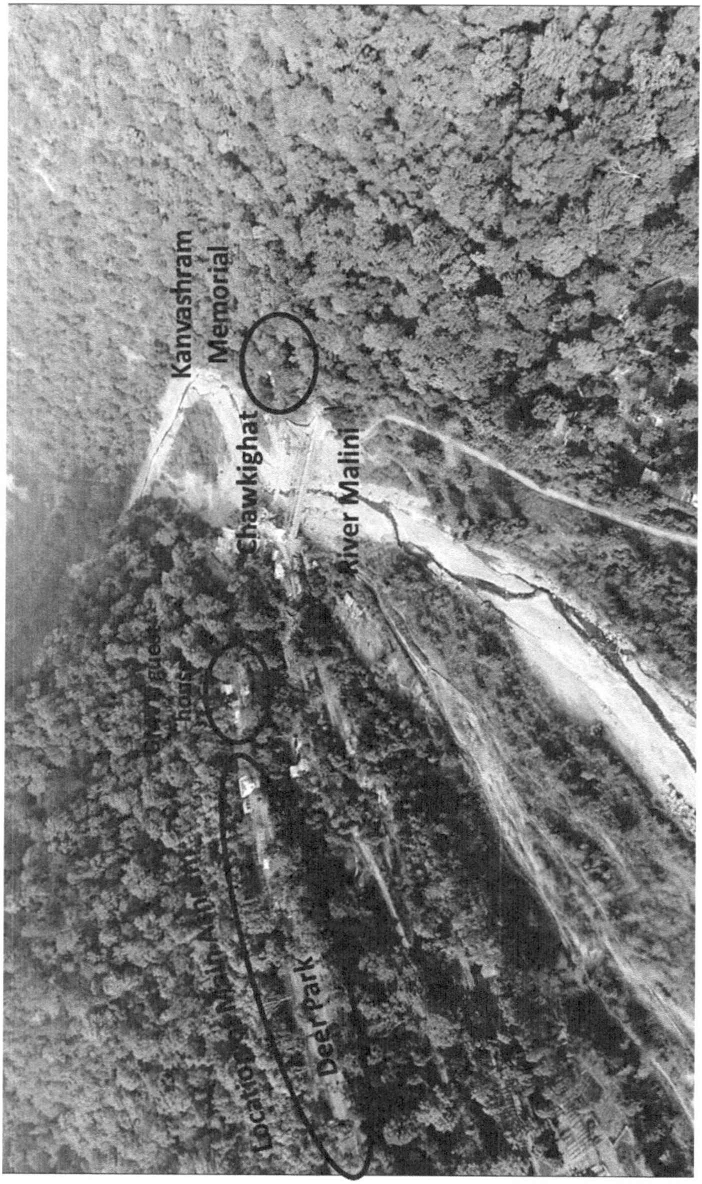

Fig 11 Drone shot of Kanvashram as it appears now

an Uttarakhand government enterprise. The guest house occupies only one hectare of land, of this tabletop. The remaining 14 hectares was fenced by the Forest Department in 1956 to create a Deer Park. The terrain of the place has not changed during the construction of the Tourist bungalow or the Deer Park. Implying that the area has not been worked upon manually or by any heavy machinery. The finding of a number of relics adjacent to the Deer Park boundary gives strength to the fact of continued habitation in the region. Kalidas in Abhigyan Shakuntalam has also described Shakuntala and her friends collecting water from the river, which point to the fact that the river must have been flowing close to the ashram.

The presence of ashram on both banks of the river as mentioned in Mahabharata is also confirmed, as there is indeed an elevated piece of about half a hectare of land, on the left bank of the river situated right opposite the main ashram, on the other bank of the river at Chawkighat. On *Basant Panchami* day in 1956, Cabinet Minister of Forest Department, Uttar Pradesh Shri Jagmohan Singh Negi, laid the foundation for the construction of a memorial on this piece of land, indicating the symbolic presence of Kanvashram. On completion, five marble statues of *rishi* Kanv, rishi Kashyap, King Dushyant, Shakuntala and Bharat with a lion were placed in the memorial. Presently only two statues of rishi Kanv and Kashyap exist in the memorial. Commemorating the day, a fair is held every year on *Basant*

Panchami, on the banks of river Malini at Chawkighat, to celebrate the occasion till date. Srinidhi Sidhalankar has also indicated that the ashram of Kanv rishi must have been located close to Chawkighat, where river Malini exits the mountainous region.

Archaeological remains and relics of ancient structures have been found time and again in the Kanvashram region. Their presence was officially put on record by ASI in 2012, after the presence of relics in the region was reported to the Director General, ASI, New Delhi by me in July 2012. **(Appendix B)** Majority of these archaeological remains have been found in a particular location, though pieces have been found lying in a radius of about a kilometre from the main site. The main site lies just outside the boundary fence of Deer Park, the area where the main ashram was located. **(Figure 23)**

Taking all the above positive indications and topography of the area into account, it is certain that the main ashram of Kanv was located close to the place where the river Malini exits the mountainous section into the plains at Chawkighat. A sizable elevated plain land next to the right bank of the river, makes it an ideal location for the establishment of an ashram. Presence of more than one habitable location in proximity to each other in the area also gives support to the fact that the ashram was spread around on various sites. Confirmation of the presence of the ashram is also authenticated by the portrayal of the ashram in the epic Mahabharat and in Abhigyan Shakuntalam. Presence of archaeological remains next to the site also confirms that the area was inhabited in the past. Though the remains found in the region pertain to ~1100 CE. Archaeological excavation has shown that the practice of building new settlements on the earlier sites is a phenomenon which has been observed in many sites excavated world-wide. In most excavated sites, a gradual time frame is revealed, by the excavated artifacts recovered. It is certain that when excavation of the Kanvashram region is done in the near future it will reveal the presence of earlier settlements.

CHAPTER 3

WHO WERE THE INHABITANTS?

Though the answer to the question, as to who were the inhabitants of Kanvashram is simple and straightforward but unfortunately historians and colonial rulers of this nation have distorted the history of this nation deliberately to such an extent, that it is a challenge to untangle the truth, from the maze of misinformation, which has been propagated over the last 200 years. Systematic and deliberate distortion of the history of this nation has been done, basically with a sinister purpose, to ensure that the coming generations of this nation, are deprived of the true and factual history of this nation, which shows that the civilisation which flourished on this subcontinent, is unbroken and continuous since its inception. All this was done with the intent, to ensure that the people of the nation Bharat Varsh, should be unaware of the fact, that the civilisation of which they are part of, was socially and culturally far advanced in all spheres, to any other civilisation, existing then on the planet. Despite the destruction of education institutes and numerous libraries, burning of tens of thousands of manuscripts by invaders and stealing of scores of manuscripts by the British colonial rulers, the Vedic culture, on which the civilisation was anchored prevailed. The credit for corrupting the history of this nation goes to Max Muller, who after becoming aware of the glorious past of this ancient civilisation, went about creating and spreading false theories, to distort the true history of this nation. It was extremely unfortunate that these bogus and fictitious theories proposed by Muller & others, were neither denounced nor challenged by the government of this nation, which took over the reign of power from the colonial rulers in 1947. They continued to disseminate the misinformation, for the next 70 years or so. These absurd theories still remain in some history books and embedded in the minds of many. New archaeological findings and research done in the nation post-independence, have brought out new facts about Sarasvati-Sindhu civilisation, which has exposed these untrue and fabricated theories.

The most prominent theory propagated by this collegium was Aryan Invasion Theory (AIT), which in simple words stated that culturally advanced and literate people, who were responsible for giving rise to Vedic culture, in the subcontinent, were not native of the land but had migrated from some unknown distant location. AIT was a politically motivated conspiracy, hatched by British colonial ruler, to undermine the culture and people of this nation. It was crafted to show that the knowledge and culture of this nation were not indigenous. Strangely, different historians propagating AIT, were amongst themselves not in agreement about the region from where these migrants had come from. The home land of these migrants in different theories is assumed in places, which are thousands of miles apart. Though all these different theories proposed, were not based on any concrete foundation, they continued to hold sway, despite protest from some Indian historians, post-independence. The dissenting voice was present but it lacked substantial proof to debunk the AIT. Pioneering excavation work done by Indian archaeologists, post-independence have unearthed new archaeological evidence along river Sarasvati and Drishadvati, which has shown that the settlements excavated along these rivers are older and in greater numbers than those close to river Indus. Indus Valley Civilisation has now rightly been addressed as Saraswati-Sindhu civilisation. Numerous research papers have been published and books written based on pioneering new excavations done in the region. However, this has not prevented some from still addressing this civilisation as Harappa or Mohenjo-Daro or Indus Valley Civilisation. Numerous fresh locations excavated in India have brought out the required proof, needed to drive the final nail in the coffin of AIT. Excavation in Rahigarhi, Sonali, Bhirrana and various other sites has proved beyond doubt that there was no migration of any kind that took place into this subcontinent. The civilisation of the sub-continent is unbroken and has been continuous since its inception in 10,000 BCE or earlier. Having put the dubious and fictitious AIT theory to rest, the Indian archaeologists and historians shifted their focus and thought process towards unearthing the full extent of Sarswati–Sindhu civilisation and its link with the Vedic culture. A considerable time and effort had been wasted to demolish the AIT theory, which could have been put to better use by the scholars. Tell-tale signs of the connection of the continued civilisation are evident but to uncover the link it is necessary to take a step at a time, into the past.

Numerous educational and spiritual centres existed in this nation which functioned under the aegis of a sage or a saint or rishi, or in other words a *Guru*. Institutions following such a system were called *Gurukul.* This traditional Vedic form of education system remained and continued to stay in existence for thousands of years since its inception. With the ingress of Mughal invaders in this subcontinent, the Vedic educational system was partially dismantled. Invading forces burnt down huge libraries in the universities of Nalanda, Takshashila etc. which were stacked with tens of thousands of ancient and precious manuscripts. Though the libraries and universities were burnt down, the prevalent education system continued to exist. It was the British colonial ruler who ultimately destroyed this ancient education system by introducing a new education system in this nation. This unscrupulous task of demolishing the existing Vedic education system was done by T. B. Macaulay. He advised the British government, that in order to destroy a civilisation, it is paramount that its existing education system is demolished. They were successful to an extent in doing so but the core ideology and concept of the Vedic education system continued to exist and could not be eradicated, as the deep-rooted cultural values remained embedded in the heart and soul of inhabitants of this nation.

Reference to the oldest ashram of this sub-continent Kanvashram, is also found in Mahabharat. Besides Kanvashram, there were many ashrams in the region, which existed in proximity and find references in different ancient scriptures. Who were the residents of Kanvashram and the other ashrams? Where had they come from? Reference to the *rishis* who lived in these ashrams is given in the oldest book of knowledge Rig Veda. As a matter of fact, it is these *rishis* and their descendants who composed the various mandals of Rig Veda.

There is no agreement amongst most historians as to where Vedas were composed, primarily Rig Veda. Different opinions are expressed, about the place and period when they were composed. These opinions, though generally accepted, are not supported by any documentary or archaeological evidence. Excavation done along the banks of river Sarasvati has not unearthed any evidence to authenticate and endorse the presence of Vedic culture. It can therefore be presumed that these are hypothetical assumptions. The hypothesis propagated has been picked up and quoted in various research papers extensively. The reason to disagree with the above assumption, is purely based on the lack of any supporting evidence, which has not been presented by anyone. Mr. BB Lal an eminent archaeologist of this nation has expressed that "Harappan and Vedic civilisation were part of the same coin." Can it be interpreted that both differed like the two sides of a coin and coexisted in the same period? They were different alright as one was an urban culture and the other rural, but they did not coexist in the same period. No physical or documentary evidence of their existence together in a particular period is available. There is also no reference in Rig Veda, which points to the fact that Vedic people lived in permanent structures made from bricks, something widely used in the construction of dwellings of the Saraswati-Sindhu civilisation. If Vedic civilisation did exist along the river Sarasvati, then there should be mention of the existence of a parallel civilisation, existing along the river Saraswati, in Rig Veda. Though there is ample reference to Sarasvati as a river and as a goddess in Rig Veda there is no mention of the fact that those who composed Rig Veda, lived along the banks of river Sarasvati. It can therefore be inferred that Sarasvati-Sindhu civilisation and Vedic civilisation did exist but in different periods and at different locations. With AIT being shelved for good, it has been proven beyond doubt that there was no migration of any outsiders into the region. It is therefore certain that the inhabitants of Sarasvati-Sindhu civilisation and Vedic culture formed part of the same continuous civilisation. In that case, the question remains as to who preceded or succeeded the other and by how much time.

Considerable information is now available about the Saraswati-Sindhu civilisation since its accidental discovery in the early 20th century. On the other hand, no physical evidence connected with Vedic civilisation has been unearthed anywhere in this subcontinent. The Saraswati-Sindhu civilisation faded away by ~1900 BCE, though the process of outwards migration of people commenced from ~2300 BCE onwards, due reduction in flow of river Sarasvati. No traces of an ashram-based system have been found in or around the city-based culture which existed mainly along the banks of river Saraswati, its tributaries and river Sindhu. So how can it be assumed that the ashram-based *rishis* were part of the Sarasvati-Sindhu civilisation, prior to its collapse? No evidence has been found in any of the numerous sites excavated, which points to the use of Sanskrit language, in which Rig Veda *shloks* are composed. A pictorial language has been found engraved on various clay tablets excavated at different locations. The mysterious language has not been deciphered, though many other ancient pictorial-based languages of different civilisations, all over the world, have been deciphered. The primary reason was that the language which originated out of the pictorial language of Sarasvati Sindhu civilisation, was also not understood. Hence none could connect the two or maybe they had no intention to do so. Prof. Yajnadevam Rao, an Indian cryptographer, based on his extensive research has concluded that the root language of Sanskrit, is the pictorial language, used by inhabitants of Sarasvati Sindhu civilisation and it has originated from it. Sanskrit language is today acclaimed and accepted as the most scientific language of the world, which was spoken by the *rishis* of Vedic civilisation. The question which comes to fore at this stage is that, if the Veda were not composed prior to the decay of the Sarasvati-Sindhu civilisation, then when and where were they composed?

The end of Saraswati-Sindhu civilisation was a gradual process, which happened over a few centuries. The continuous reduction in flow of the river Sarasvati, gave inhabitants living on its bank, sufficient time to move to new destinations. The inhabitants of this vast civilisation gradually spread out in different directions. Outward migration happened in a phased manner and the majority of inhabitants moved upstream, along the drying and receding river Saraswati. Others moved to settle on the bank of river Drishadvati, which had reasonable flow in its bed. However, the water in river Drishadvati disappeared subsequently, forcing the migrants to move once again. The movement of migrants is indicated by the increase in settlement upstream of river Sarasvati and along the banks of river Drishadvati. Dating of excavated sites along rivers has corroborated this fact.

The psychology of human behaviour generally functions in an identical manner, irrespective of which part or region of the earth they belong to. When things and situations are favourable the humans enjoy and make merry. They do not for once comprehend that circumstances can dramatically change in the future, due to some unforeseen reason and are not prepared for any impending transformation. Conditions change rapidly when natural disasters strike. An earthquake, a flood, a volcanic eruption or a tsunami can destroy everything and alter the complete topography of a region. These events can neither be predicted nor can they be precisely forecasted even now in the 21st century. The few who survive the event, having lost all, migrate to new locations. These extremely violent events have at times wiped out complete civilisation or population of a region. The drying up of river Sarasvati was a catastrophic event, which ruined a well-entrenched mature civilisation, which has been evolving on its banks. No loss of human life occurred due to this unforeseen event. This fact has been thoroughly researched and no traces of violent death of inhabitants have been observed in human remains excavated in various sites, either due to natural calamity or violence unleashed by external invaders. This therefore rules out the ingress of any external invaders from distant land into the subcontinent, who clashed with inhabitants of Sarasvati-Sindhu civilisation and overpowered them. It therefore endorses the fact that no external invaders entered the boundaries of this nation and hence negates the dubious Aryan Invasion Theory. The maturing of a civilisation is a slow process which occurs over thousands of years. From its initial beginning, the Sarasvati-Sindhu civilisation reached its mature phase in ~2700 BCE, with the emergence of the urban phase of civilisation. This mature phase lasted till ~2300 BCE. The civilisation thereafter started to disintegrate, though the ultimate collapse of the civilisation happened by ~1300 BCE.

A civilisation is generally presumed to be a homogenous setup. This may not be true. As the population of a settlement increases it gradually spreads out over a wide area and ultimately gets divided into various subgroups. These subgroups in time exhibit different levels of economic, social and cultural development. The same can be observed even in present modern societies. Disparity develops between different groups over a period, more so at the economic level. Nations in the past and even today, are at different levels of development. Within a nation itself, the inhabitants cannot be considered at par with each other, economically or intellectually. Sarasvati-Sindhu civilisation in time spread out over a very vast area, estimated to be about 100,000 sq. km or more during its mature phase, with its inhabitants living in small and big habitats. This mammoth area of the civilisation is arrived, based on the presently excavated sites, which existed at different periods. Some sites display an urban culture but majority display a semi-urban or rural-based life, like that which still exists in this nation. A diverse and widely spread civilisation, also exhibits different intellect levels. Some groups become intellectually advanced possessing greater knowledge about their environment and surroundings. With a better understanding of the prevalent situation, these groups can anticipate the changes, which may take place in the future. The reduction in rainfall in the region and reduced flow of water in river Sarasvati must have been observed by all the inhabitants. Groups with a better understanding of the environmental situation must have been the first to move out of their permanent abode. It is an extremely stressful and distressing decision, to abandon a permanent settlement, more so if the inhabitants and their ancestors have been living there for thousands of years. Those groups who were knowledgeable must have migrated out to newer locations, earlier than the rest. There must have been many early starters. Depending upon the information available within the group, their internal decisions and conflicts, the groups must have migrated in different directions. The earliest movement of the inhabitants commenced by ~2300 BCE. Did some of the wise men and women move East? If they did, they had a choice to select from several rivers that existed east of river Sarasvati and settle down on their banks. All rivers that existed then, in that period are still flowing.

What is of concern to us at this juncture are those inhabitants who moved East of river Saraswati. It is possible that the groups which migrated Eastward, had some knowledge of the terrain and of the various major or minor rivers flowing in the region. It is equally possible that they learnt about the terrain and presence of rivers, as they shifted from one location to another. At some juncture, they must have found a suitable site and settled down, based on their necessity and requirements. Those who found the right environment must have prospered. Others after a brief stay may have continued to migrate. Some unfortunate groups may have perished. Where exactly did those who moved eastward from Sarasvati-Sindhu civilisation settle down?

A number of *shloks* (verses/hymn/*stuka*) in Rig Veda shower praise on seven rivers, though the rivers are not mentioned collectively by name, in any *shlok,* in Mandal 2 to 9 of Rig Veda. Mostly one river is mentioned but in some *shlok,* two rivers are mentioned by different composers. Few *shlok* refer to seven rivers. The seven major rivers could be Saraswati, Sindhu, Beas, Sutlej, Ravi, Jhelum and Chanab. Some tributaries of river Sindhu are also mentioned in Rig Veda. Sarasvati is mentioned maximum number of times as a river. In some *shloks* river Sarasvati is referred to as a goddess and in other places as a mother. Were the *shloks* of Rig Veda composed along the bank of any of these seven rivers? It is not certain, as none of the *shlok* give any indication of the location, where they were composed or the period when they were composed. Verses of Rig Veda are considered by most scholars to have been composed around ~1500 BCE. If the date is accepted as a datum, then the only major noticeable event available on record in the ancient documents, which is known to have occurred, before or concurrently with the composing of the *shloks* of Rig Veda, is enumerated in Mahabharat. It is the birth and coronation of Emperor Bharat. Mahabharat war, which took place between Pandav and Kaurav, occurred sometime between 1100 and 1200 BCE as per the findings of the Archaeological Survey of India, based on available data and excavation. Emperor Bharat, son of King Dushyant and Shakuntala was born 16 generations prior to the great war. **(Figure 03)** This places his birth approximately about ~480 years plus or minus 100, before the great war i.e. between 1600 to 1700 BCE.

A void of information exists between the commencement of disintegration of the Sarasvati-Sindhu civilisation in ~2300 BCE and the birth of Emperor Bharat. A period of about 600 to 700 years is unaccounted for, about which limited information is available in the present historical books. However, Mahabharat covers this period by describing the Bharat/Puru lineage. **(Figure 12)** The lineage starts from Daksh. Emperor Bharat, in the generation chart is placed 25 generations after Daksh i.e. after a period of about ~750 years. To say that nothing was happening or happened during those years will be erroneous. The inhabitants who were forced to migrate from the banks of river Sarasvati, and moved eastward and settled in the region east of river Ganga, had the record of their ancestors and the same appears in epic Mahabharat. The knowledge migrants who abandoned the banks of river Sarasvati were carrying a thought, a concept with them, which continued to grow in the coming future and laid the foundation of a new culture in the subcontinent.

Migrating eastwards, from the banks of river Saraswati, some migrants reached river Malini, a tributary of river Ganga. It is quite likely that they could be those who had shifted earlier and resettled along the bank of river Drishadvati and had to move again as the river dried out subsequently. The arial distance between the two rivers, Sarasvati and Malini, is about 400–500 km.

On the other hand, those who had migrated upstream of river Sarasvati had no necessity to move as river Sarasvati still had water in its bed upstream. The distance may have been covered in a phased manner or in one go. It cannot be said with certainty whether the migrants reached the shores of river Malini based on some previous knowledge or they just stumbled on the said location by chance but it is abundantly clear that the decision to establish the ashram, on the banks of river Malini, was made based on careful analysis of the topography of the region and various other environmental factors. This movement and ultimate settlement could have happened sometime between 2300 and 1900 BCE. Did the river Malini on whose banks the migrants settled had a name then? It is extremely unlikely. It is also unlikely that the two major rivers Ganga and Jamuna,

Family Tree (Bharat Lineage)

Daksh
Aditi
Vivasvan
Manu
Ila
Pururava
Ayu
Nahush

Sharmishta -------- m ------- Yayati --------- m -------- Devayani

Sharmishta's children: Druhyu, Anu, Puru – m- Koushalya

Devayani's children: Turvasu, Yadu

Janamejay – m – Ananta
Prachinvan – m – Ashamki
Snayati – m – Varangi
Ahanyati – m – Bhanumati
Sarvabhoum – m – Sunanda
Jayatsen—m –Sushrava
Avachin – m – Maryada
Mahabhoum – m –Suyagya
Ayutanayi – m – Kama
Akrodhn – m – Karambha
Devatithi – m – Marayda
Arih – m – Sudeva
Riksh – m – Jvala
Matinar – m – Sarasvati
Tansu – m – Kalindi
Illin – m – Rathantari
Dushyant – m – Shakuntala
Bharat – m – Sunanda

Fig 12 Bharat-Puru Family Lineage

which the migrants had crossed to reach river Malini, had a name. Though the Sarasvati Sindhu civilisation came up on the bank of river Sarasvati, there is no indication that the rivers were addressed as Sarasvati and Sindhu then. Majority of the names of rivers flowing in this subcontinent presently known to us, are in Sanskrit. The names of the individual rivers convey a meaning and indicate the character of the river. The naming of the various rivers was done in the years preceding the composition of Rig Veda when the Sanskrit language was evolving and taking shape. An advanced language like Sanskrit must have taken years to develop but with the right gathering of innovative individuals, it could have evolved in a few decades or maybe in a century or two from the root language used by the migrants. All this must have happened within 600–700 years, as this is the time interval between the moving of the inhabitants from the bank of river Sarasvati and the establishment of Kanvashram on the bank of river Malini. Why the river Malini was chosen is discussed in the succeeding chapter.

Having found a suitable place, it must have taken some time for the migrants to create a favourable environment to pursue a steady life. Settled comfortably in the new conducive environment, the elders of the group who had suffered the pain of displacement must have been haunted by the trauma of displacement they had gone through, in abandoning their well-settled homeland. They must have recollected and recited innumerable tales of the glorious past, spent along the banks of river Sarasvati, to the younger generation. The information was passed down from father to son and from *Guru* to disciples. In this new stable environment along the bank of river Malini, with plenty of food, water and a stable environment, a new culture took root. This new culture took about 600 to 700 years to mature. The evolution of the Sanskrit language, the stories of the glorious past and understanding of the present, were remoulded from prose into poetry, as they are easy to memorize. The poems were subsequently converted and composed into *shloks*. The settlers on the bank of river Malini, thereafter went on to conceive and fashion an educational system. Were these settlers responsible for establishing a new culture, which is now called Vedic and composed the Rig Veda? If it is so, we must gather more information about this new culture.

Different opinions and theories are propagated about the places where Vedic civilisation or culture originated. As these assumptions have thrived unchallenged for a long time, they have been blindly accepted. The theories basically state that some people, for some unknown reason, migrated from some far-off distant land into this subcontinent and created the Vedic culture. The location suggested by different scholars and historians is spread all over. The places include Swat valley in Pakistan, river Helmand in Afghanistan, the region around Caspian Sea in Central Asia, the region between river Sarasvati and Drishadvati and finally the most accepted, North West Punjab in India. There could be many more. Besides the location, the time of existence of the Vedic civilisation has also not been clearly defined.

River Swat rises in the Hindi-Kush range which lies in the northern mountainous region of present-day Pakistan. The river is called *Suvastu* in Sanskrit. The valley through which the river flows, is considered by some to be the place of origin of Vedic culture. From the present archaeological find, the valley in the recent past was a predominantly Buddhist settlement, as the place is littered with Buddhist iconic statues and remains. As per the hypothesis proposed, the Vedic culture originated and flourished in the lush and fertile valley of the river Swat. Isolated from outside influence and with plenty of water, the region can sustain and support a reasonable population though the weather of the valley turns bitterly cold in the winter months with heavy snowfall for six months. If the Swat valley inhabitants were the creators of Vedic culture who subsequently did migrate to this subcontinent, some reference about the region should have existed in the Rig Veda or some other ancient documents.

The second hypothesis proposes that Vedic civilisation originated on the banks of river Helmand. The river originates in the Hindu Kush and flows in Afghanistan. The region through which the river flows is fertile. A civilisation did take root on the banks of the river but that was sometime in the 3rd century BCE. The people who settled there must have migrated westward after the collapse of the Sarasvati Sindhu civilisation and settled there. Hence for all practical purposes the civilisation that came up along the river Helmand valley, cannot be considered a Vedic civilisation.

Yet another theory proposed designates the places of origin of Vedic culture to a region around the Caspian Sea. This hypothesis was circulated by those who are also credited with crafting the dubious Aryan Invasion or Migration Theory, which propagated that migration occurred into the Indian subcontinent, from a distant land by people who were culturally advanced than the existing inhabitants. These migrants were labelled as Aryan. The word *Aryan* has been crafted from Sanskrit word *Arya*, which was used to address an individual. This dubious Aryan Invasion Theory has been set aside by most today. Most researchers and historians of the 19th century considered that a civilisation existed along the river Sindhu, as it was the major river flowing in that region in that period. The initial excavated sites like Mohenjo-Daro and Harappa, happen to lie close to river Indus (Sindhu). They thus named it the Indus Valley civilisation. All the researchers, explorers, Indologist etc., were unaware of the fact that the civilisation was actually located along the banks of the mighty river Sarasvati, which once flowed in the region and had gone extinct. It was only in the early 20th century, that the existence of the extinct river Sarasvati came to light and by the end of the 20th century, it was established beyond doubt that the largest river which ever flowed in this subcontinent, was river Sarasvati. The river originated from the Bandar Poonch glaciers of Himalayas in Uttarakhand, India. The river exited the mountains at Adi Badri, Himachal Pradesh. It flowed past the plains of Punjab, Rajasthan and ultimately flowed into the Arabian Sea at Rann of Kutch. The only movement of people that took place in the subcontinent was by inhabitants of Sarasvati-Sindhu civilisation, due to drying of the river Saraswati. It was due to outward migration of people from the region, that the seed of knowledge was sown, all over the world. With the ceremonial demise of the AIT, the theory of the imaginary origin of the Vedic people in Central Asia, circulated by some, can also be discarded.

The fourth place up for consideration is the region that lies between the river Sarasvati and its tributary Drishadvati. Opinions are expressed that the Vedic culture originated in this region and the *rishis* who composed the various mandals of the Rig Veda lived there. The area which lies between the two rivers was part of the Sarasvati-Sindhu civilisation, and is confirmed by the presence of numerous sites excavated there. If the Vedic culture did exist in that region, it should have coexisted with the Sarasvati Sindhu civilisation. However, it does not find any mention in the archaeological research and reports published about the region or vice versa no reference to the Sarasvati Sindhu civilisation exists in the Rig Veda. Measured by any yardstick Vedic culture was different, using an advanced language Sanskrit. Besides, both had a different way of living. Vedic culture was rural, ashram based while the other urban or semi-urban. A fairly large number of disparities exist between the two and with no documentary proof available it is unlikely that they could have coexisted. They must have flourished at different locations and times. The drying river Sarasvati forced the settlers to migrate. Most moved upstream along the receding river Sarasvati but some moved and resettled on the banks of river Drishadvati flowing South of it. Archaeological excavations have shown that there was an increase in the number of settlements, along the river Drishadvati upper reaches, post 2300 BCE. Continuous lean monsoon spell that persisted for ~900 years in the region from 2350 to 1450 BCE resulted in reduced flow of water in river Drishadvati and compelled the migrants to move yet again. The river Drishadvati does find a single mention in Rig Veda 3.23.4. We now have abundant information available about the Sarasvati-Sindhu civilisation, thanks to the excavation done by dedicated archaeologists of the nation, post-independence. A boost has been given to continue the research by the government led by Prime Minister Shri Narendra Modi, post 2014. However, no evidence has been put forward that the Vedic culture coexisted with the Sarasvati Sindhu civilisation. One final issue that needs mention is that, none of the rishi's mentioned in Rig Veda lived in this region, as no information is documented in any epic or ancient text about their presence in the region. However, there is a possibility that the people who ultimately migrated out from this region were responsible for the creation of the Vedic civilisation in the subcontinent.

A fairly large number of present-day scholars consider that the North-West (NW) Punjab region in India was the centre of Vedic culture. It is an established fact, that majority of the inhabitants of the Sarasvati Sindhu civilisation did move northwards upstream and settled along the receding and drying river Sarasvati, a fact corroborated by the excavated settlements found along the river Sarasvati. The upper reaches of the river Sarasvati where the settlements have been found lie in south Punjab and the northern part of Haryana. Earlier the complete region was called Punjab, meaning land of five rivers Jhelum, Chenab, Ravi, Beas and Sutlej. With no migration from outside, the migrants from the Sarasvati Sindhu civilisation, who settled there must have created a new culture in the region. Hence, in all probability the hypothesis about Vedic culture having originated in the NW Punjab holds ground. This advanced civilisation, must have matured over a period of ~ 700 years. A new language was crafted and *shloks* were composed praising river Sarasvati and various gods, who had taken shape over the years amongst this new culture. However, one question still lingers and needs to be answered, to confirm the origin of the Vedic culture in this region. North-West Punjab is a vast area through which river Sarasvati flowed. Where exactly did the Rishi and their descendants who composed the various mandals of Rigveda had their ashrams located? In some ancient documents, the *rishis* mentioned in Rig Veda have been identified with some specific locations but none of these locations are in NW Punjab region. Clearly, none of the rishis or their descendants who composed the Rig Veda ever lived in NW Punjab region. However, it cannot be ruled out that ancestors of these *rishis* who composed the Rig Veda, have migrated from NW Punjab or the region which lies between river Sarasvati and Drishadvati to the place where the Vedic culture ultimately sprouted. The story does not end here. There is one last lead that can provide answers to all the missing links and bring us to the cradle of the Vedic culture, where it blossomed, matured and flourished and where the hymns of Rig Veda were composed.

Humans have been forever mesmerised by the power and influence of various natural forces like fire, thunder, rain, wind etc., and their effect on all beings living on this planet. They have observed the blessing and destructive effect unleashed by these natural forces but found themselves helpless in controlling them. They were neither able to reduce or increase the effect of these forces. Unable to overpower these natural forces, humans elevated them to a higher pedestal and ultimately gave them divine status. They offered prayers and composed *shloks* praising these powerful forces of nature like *Agni* (Fire), *Indra* (Rain), *Vayu* (Air), thunder and other forces, to pacify them, to reduce their destructive effect. *Shloks* were composed and chanted while seated around a fireplace. Offerings were made to these divine forces to subdue them or to bring them into effect. The complete concept of *Yagya* originated from these fireplaces, where the fire must have been kept burning, for the people living in the cluster to obtain fire from that source. Subsequently, the *Havan Kund* (fire place) was made a pious place and *Yagya* and various other sacred rituals carried out around it. The *shloks* composed were verbally passed down generations and this continued for a long period of time. At some stage, the *shloks* composed by different *rishis* and their descendants were consolidated and written down. The ancient document thus created was called Rig Veda *Sahita*. The word *sahita,* is a collection or assimilation of works of different composers. The assimilation of *shloks* may have been done by an individual or a group of people. Rig Veda is presently considered to be the oldest written document on this planet. Rig Veda, available today, in print is composed of 10 *Mandals* (chapters). There are multiple references to river Sarasvati in Rig Veda. Sarasvati is referred to as a river (RgV 3.23.4, 3.33.1, 4.41.16 etc.), as mother (RgV 2.4.15-17) and as a goddess along with Bharti and Ila (RgV 2.3.8, 3.4.8, 5.5.8, etc.) in *Mandals* from 2 to 9. Of the 10 *Mandals* in the Rig Veda, *Mandals* 1 and 10 are later additions to the original text and this is evident from the description of some geographical narrative in those *Mandals.* In *Mandals* 2 to 9 river Sarasvati is described as the noisiest and mightiest of all rivers flowing in the region (RgV 6.61.1 to14) but in mandal 10 the status of the largest and the fastest flowing river is bestowed to river Sindhu (RgV 10.75.7). This clearly shows that there is a time difference between the composition of *Mandal* 1 and10 and *Mandals* 2 to 9. The strength and flow of river Sarasvati reduced drastically after Sutlej deserted it and joined Beas, a tributary of Sindhu. With additional water received, the flow of river Sindhu was greatly enhanced, making it the largest river in the region. This disparity between the strength of the two rivers described clearly indicates a time-lapse. The *shloks* of Rig Veda were composed over a long period and penned down at a later date. Plenty of assorted information is available in this ancient document. To get any meaningful micro information is difficult but some major conclusions can be inferred from the *shloks* written.

Mandal 2 to 9 of Rig Veda are credited to *rishis* Grtsmada, Visvamitra, Vamdev, Atri, Bharadwaj, Vasishta, Kanv and Kashyap respectively. The descendants of these eight *rishis* continued to add *shloks* to the original composition. Though most *shloks* praise the natural forces, some provide geographical details about the vast Northern region of the subcontinent. Seven rivers have been referred to many times in *Mandals* 2 to 9 (RgV 2.12.13, 4.28.1, 8.69.12 etc.), though none of the *rishis* have mentioned the names of these rivers collectively. Seven rivers mentioned individually in different *shloks* could be, Sarasvati, Sindhu, Sutlej, Ravi, Beas, Chenab and Jhelum, though they may or may not have been connected at that time. Six of these rivers are connected presently. Sarasvati was a river with Sutlej as its tributary, which later changed its course. Thus, it gives rise to the possibility that the seven rivers mentioned, may refer to the tributaries of river Saraswati. "River Sarasvati flows down with her seven sisters having greater speed and flow as compared to other rivers" (RgV 6.61.9). In that case, these seven rivers would be Drishadvati, Markenda, Dangri, Ghaggar, Sutlej, Jammuna and Wah. It is equally possible that the seven rivers could be a combination of some other rivers which could have been tributaries of river Sarasvati. Some of the names of these rivers have changed over the years but most rivers are still addressed by their original name. The correct geographical sequence of the rivers flowing in the North India region has been scripted at a later period, in *Mandal* 10 of Rig Veda. The major rivers flowing from East to West have been identified as *Ganga, Jamuna, Saraswati, Shatudari* (Sutlej), *Parushshani* (Ravi), *Ashakani* (Chanab), *Ajirkia* (Beas), *Vitsata* (Jhelum) and *Sindhu* (Indus), (RgV 10.75.5). This clearly shows that the rishis who composed the various *Mandals* of the Rig Veda, were familiar with the topography of the region as far West up to river Sindu and as far East as the river Ganga. The actual sequence of the rivers in the northern region was assimilated by them at a much later date when the rivers were given names in Sanskrit .

From Rig Veda, it can be inferred that the ashram of the eight *rishis* who composed *Mandals* 2 to 9, must have been in proximity. They must have resided in a particular region, in the same time-period and were interacting with each other. Also, their succeeding generations must have continued to maintain close ties with each other. This is confirmed by the fact that the subjects addressed by the different *rishis* in Rig Veda are alike and the style of composition of *shloks* is the same. Strangely though, Rig Veda does not reveal the location of the ashram of the rishis. Other ancient documents also do not disclose much, but then there is always an exception. The presence and location of the ashram of one rishi amongst the eight is documented. Details of the ashram and location of this one rishi are scripted in an ancient document. The 8th *Mandal* of the Rig Veda is composed by *rishi* KANV, and the ashram in which he resided with his innumerable disciples was called Kanvashram. The *ashram* of *rishi* Kanv was located on the banks of river Malini. This fact, in no uncertain terms, is enumerated in Mahabharat. Besides the description of the great war in Mahabharat, the only other story which does not have a mythological element in it is the story of King Dushyant and Shakuntala and the birth of Emperor Bharat in Kanvashram. Hence, the place where rishi Kanv had his *ashram* is clearly and factually identified, to have existed on the bank of river Malini. River Malini still flows and is a tributary of river Ganga. Having identified the abode Kanvashram of *rishi* Kanv, the next step is to locate the ashrams of the other *rishis* mentioned in the Rig Veda. Where did the other seven rishis live? They must have had their ashrams close to Kanvashram.

One of the leads that can be followed in solving the puzzle, involves two *rishis* Vishvamitra and Vasistha. Numerous stories in the Puranas and other ancient texts portray the tussle between Vishvamitra and Vasistha, with each one described as trying to subdue the other on different occasions. Who finally prevailed is not certain and is not an issue in the present context, as each story tells a different tale. The active verbal or physical duel between the two must have been only possible if both rishis were living in the same period and in the same region. Both these *rishis* have been credited to have composed a *Mandal* of the Rig Veda. The 3rd Mandal is credited to Vishvamitra and 7th Mandal to *rishi* Vasistha. Adding another link to the chain, *rishi* Kanv and Visvamitra are also known to have existed in the same period. Their presence together is described in Mahabharat and in Abhigyan Shakuntalam. The composer of the second *Mandal* of Rig Veda is Grtsmada. In a story in Mahabharat, rishi Vasistha curses Grtsmada for faltering in recitation of some text. This indicates that either they had an altercation amongst themselves or that rishi Vasistha was possibly the guru of Grtsmada and had scolded him. Grtsmada must have at a later period, achieved the status of a *rishi*, as *Mandal* 2 of the Rig Veda is composed by him. From the preceding interaction described between the rishis, it is abundantly clear that the four rishis Kanv, Vishvamitra, Vasistha and Grtsmada were living in the same region and must have had their ashram in proximity. Out of the four, the geographical location of one can be authentically and truly confirmed and that is of rishi Kanv. Shakuntala was the daughter of *rishi* Visvamitra and was brought up by rishi Kanv in his ashram. Even till date, a place close to Kanvashram, is called Vistar Katil **(Figure 14)** "depicted in next chapter", which local residents of the region refer to as the place where Vishwamitra's ashram was located. The place is about 4 km upstream from Kanvashram, in the dense jungle adjacent to river Malini. Another place close to Kanvashram is addressed as Kasayali, in the region. It is referred to by local residents as the place where the ashram of rishi Kashyap was located. *Rishi* Kashyap is the composer of the 9th *Mandal* of the Rig Veda. The highest mountain peak Hemkut (5600 ft) in the region, lying about 4 km North of Kanvashram is also referred to as the place where the ashram of rishi Kashyap was located. Besides the five *rishis* already discussed, whereabouts of the other three rishis Vamdev, Atri and Bharadwaj is not found in any ancient scriptures but as they are amongst the eight *rishis* who composed the original text (*Mandal* 2 to 9) of Rig Veda, they in all probability must have lived in the same region, having their ashram in proximity to Kanvashram.

Taking all the above into consideration, it can be surmised that the Vedic culture was crafted by the ancestors of these eight *rishis* and propagated by their descendants. The new culture which came into being in this subcontinent matured and blossomed along the banks of river Malini.

The raw concept or the seed of this culture was carried by a group of people, who migrated out from the region which lies between river Drishadvati and Sarasvati or possibly those who lived on the banks of receding river Sarasvati in Punjab. The *rishis,* who were ultimately responsible for creating this unique advanced culture, were the descendants of these migrants. The Vedic culture grew and matured over a period of about ~600 years consequent to the collapse of the Sarasvati Sindhu civilisation. The region around the banks of river Malini provided the perfect surroundings, in terms of stable environment conditions, weather and steady availability of water, conditions necessary for any civilisation to take root, blossom and mature. The ancestors of various *rishis* who settled along the river Malini and established their ashram around Kanvashram, also established the first Vedic education system in the world. This system of education spread around and was responsible for the creation of hundreds of thousands of education centres in this subcontinent, called *Gurukul.* This system of education existed and flourished in this nation for three millennia, till it was partially destroyed by the colonial occupiers. It was these rishis or their ancestors who composed the initial *shloks* of Rig Veda. The descendants of the *rishis* continued to compose and add *shloks* to the original text, which were orally passed down the generations. The *shloks* were assimilated and written down later and the first Veda came into being. The book, with 10 *Mandals,* 1028 *Stukas* and

10,600 *shloks*, credited to eight rishis, who were descendants of the migrants of the Sarasvati Sindhu civilisation, was called Rig Veda *Sahita*.

River Malini still flows in the state of Uttarakhand in India. With innumerable ancient temples and religious shrines, Uttarakhand is the Land of the Gods or in other words, the wise and knowable being, called *rishis*. The oldest and revered Hindu shrines Badri and Kedar Dham, are located on the snow-covered mountain ranges of Himalaya, along with innumerable holy shrines scattered all over Uttarakhand. It is therefore not surprising that since time immemorial people from all over the world have been flocking to this land to gain spiritual knowledge, passed down the generations, by the creator of the Vedic culture, which thrived here. In all this, at the focal point of this newly evolved Vedic culture was Kanvashram. A centre of education, culture and spirituality. Close to Kanvashram lies a place called Charak which is identified with *rishi* Charak, the author of Charak Sahita. A book that defines the basic concept of Ayurvedic medicine. Though *rishi* Charak lived in a much later period in ~300 BCE, his presence in the region indicates a continuity of the Vedic culture. Even till today Charak hamlet exists surrounded by dense jungle, rich in numerous medicinal plants. (**Figure 14**) "depicts the map of these locations, provided in the next chapter."

CHAPTER 4

WHY MALINI?

A question that surfaces in the mind of anyone doing some serious research on Kanvashram is, why did the ancestors of *rishi* Kanv, choose the banks of river Malini. They surely must have had numerous reasons to do so. What the ancestors of *rishi* Kanv thought, under the then-existing circumstances and what were their priorities, can never be fully known but a systematic and reasonable analysis of the river and its surrounding environment can lead us to some positive conclusion, however strange they might seem. It is difficult to figure out, what our ancestors must have envisaged ~4,000 years ago. It is possible, that their way of thinking and reasoning was not very different, from how we logically analyse things today, before selecting a new location to settle down. When exactly rational thinking in humans evolved, cannot be said with certainty but it has happened not so long ago, compared to the total span of human existence. Change in thinking must have taken place, with change in living conditions and circumstances but overall the vast majority still think and behave in the same way, as they possibly did in the recent past. Therefore, it is most likely that the knowledgeable migrants must have considered all aspects, like availability of food, water, security of the clan, safe shelter etc., before deciding to settle down on the banks of the river Malini.

An inseparable bond exists between the river Malini and Kanvashram. All references to Kanvashram in ancient documents and in Mahabharat have related Kanvashram to the river Malini. Foreign travellers and visitors who visited this nation on different occasions have referred to river Malini in their memoirs. A Greek explorer, historian and traveller Megasthane who visited the court of Emperor Chandra Gupt Maurya, has in his book Indica, written about the importance of the river Malini. Based on fragments of the book available, a paragraph was included in the official gazette of the Uttar Pradesh, India, published by the colonial ruler of this nation, highlighting the importance of the river. **(Figure 04)**

Alexander Cunningham, CSI Director General of Archaeological Survey of India, in his book "The Ancient Geography of India" has written "*It seems probable that the people of Mandawar as pointed out by M. Vivien de St. Martin may be the Mathoe of Magesthanese who dwelt on the banks of Erineses. If so, that river must be Malini. It is true that this is but a small stream, but it was in a sacred grove on the bank of Malini that Shakuntala was brought up and along its course lay her route to the court of Dushyanta at Hustinapur. While the lotus floats on its river and while Chakwa calls its mate on its bank, so long will the little Malini live in the verses of Kalidas."*

Considering the detailed description of Kanvashram, on the bank of river Malini, provided in Mahabharata and references in other documents, it is possible to infer that the ashram of sage Kanv (Kanvashram) was located on the bank of river Malini. Malini is but a small tributary of the river Ganga (Ganges). Cascading from the folds of Shivalik mountain, it flows into river Ganga, considered the holiest river, by all who presently reside in this nation. The other significant river is River Jamuna flows parallel and to the West of river Ganga. Both these rivers merge a few hundred kilometres downstream in Prayagraj (old name Allahabad), in the state of Uttar Pradesh. There are many other minor rivers flowing in the region besides Malini. These are Soan, Song, Pili Nadi, Ravasan, Sukro and Khoh (a tributary of Ramganga), Khosi, Gaula, Ramganga etc. **(Figure 13)** All are tributaries of the river Ganga and merges into it at different locations. With so many rivers, big and small to choose from, what compelling reason forced the ancestors of sage Kanv to settle on the bank of the river Malini?

Most human settlements are primarily established on the bank of the river or close to a water body, as it provides an uninterrupted supply of fresh water to the residents around the year, primarily for drinking, irrigation and other basic necessities. This is so, as survival and the very existence

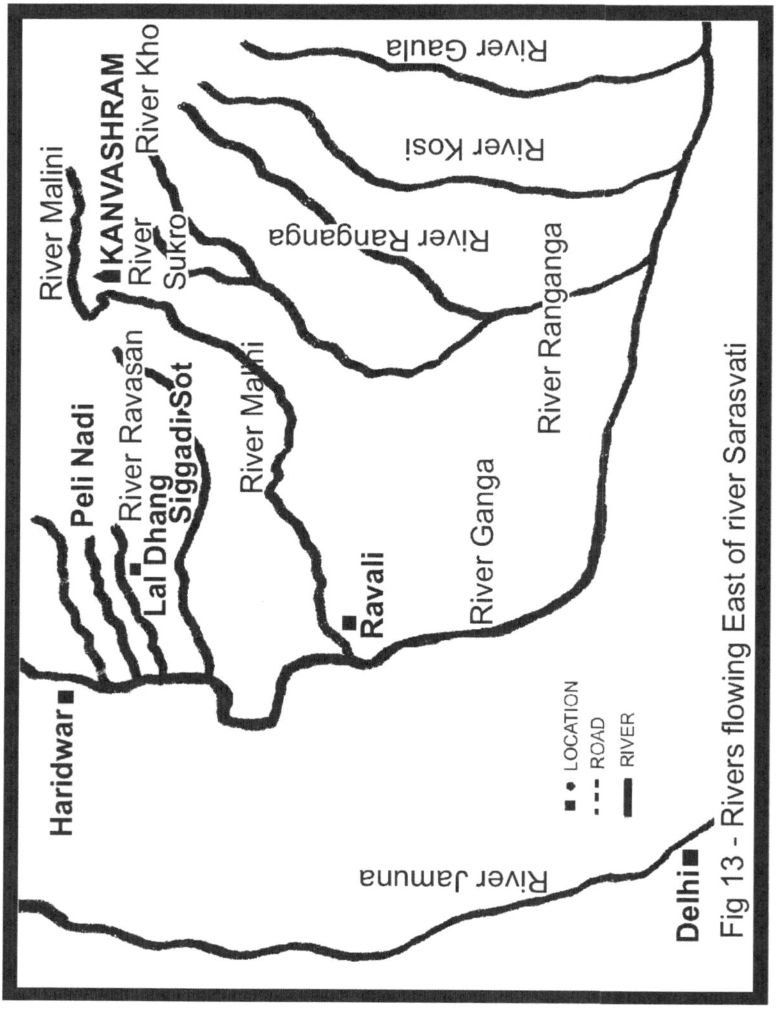

Fig 13 - Rivers flowing East of river Sarasvati

of humans depend on water. The water of river Malini, still as of today, is refreshing and sweet to drink. It is possible that the clear, cool, sweet and gentle flowing water of the river Malini, must have drawn the ancestors of sage Kanv to its banks. Though it is certain, the water of the other rivers flowing in the region must have been equally pure and drinkable during that period, rivers that are glacier-fed tend to discharge muddied water on two distinct occasions. Once during the monsoon period and other during the summer months when the melting glaciers feed into the river. As Malini is not a glacier-fed river, hence its water stays muddied only for a brief period during the monsoon. However, during monsoon season, a number of natural springs sprout in the region, which provide crystal clear drinkable water. Presently also, a number of natural springs exist around the Kanvashram region, which discharge clean water throughout the year. In case of disruption of water supply, residents of this region still rely on these natural springs. Besides the availability of clean water round the year there must surely be other factors, which compelled the migrants to decide in her favour. Dense forest on both banks of the river still exists and so do fruit and flower trees at some locations. The fruit trees may have come up naturally or could have been planted by someone. Abundant growth of medicinal plants and herbs is observed in the forest of Malini valley and in the surrounding jungle. It can be considered a reason, in present-day thinking but did the migrants possess the knowledge to harness these plants for medicinal use then, is not certain.

Ancestors of sage Kanv were uprooted from their permanent settlement, due to the drying up of the river Sarasvati, on whose bank they resided. The decision to choose a new settlement, from the numerous rivers flowing in the region, was based on one crucial factor, that their coming generation should not suffer the same fate of displacement, due disappearance of the life-giving river. Malini must have been evaluated on factors that contributed to the drying up of the river Sarasvati. Before we continue, it would be appropriate to know more about the fortunate Malini, on whose bank ultimately ancestors of sage Kanv settled and where Vedic culture sprouted and Kanvashram came up as the very first educational and spiritual institute of this nation and the world. This subcontinent was not addressed as Baharat Varsh then.

Shivalik range is one of the mountain ranges of the Himalayas. The range lies south of the Greater Himalayas and the average height of the mountain does not exceed 2000 m. Numerous rivers emerge from the folds of this range, which provide water to the vast population of the Northern region of this nation. One of these rivers is Malini, which spouts out of the earth at a place called Chandakhal, near village- Malinya, Patti - Ajmer, Block-Duggada, Dist-Pauri Garhwal, Uttarakhand, India. The place where the

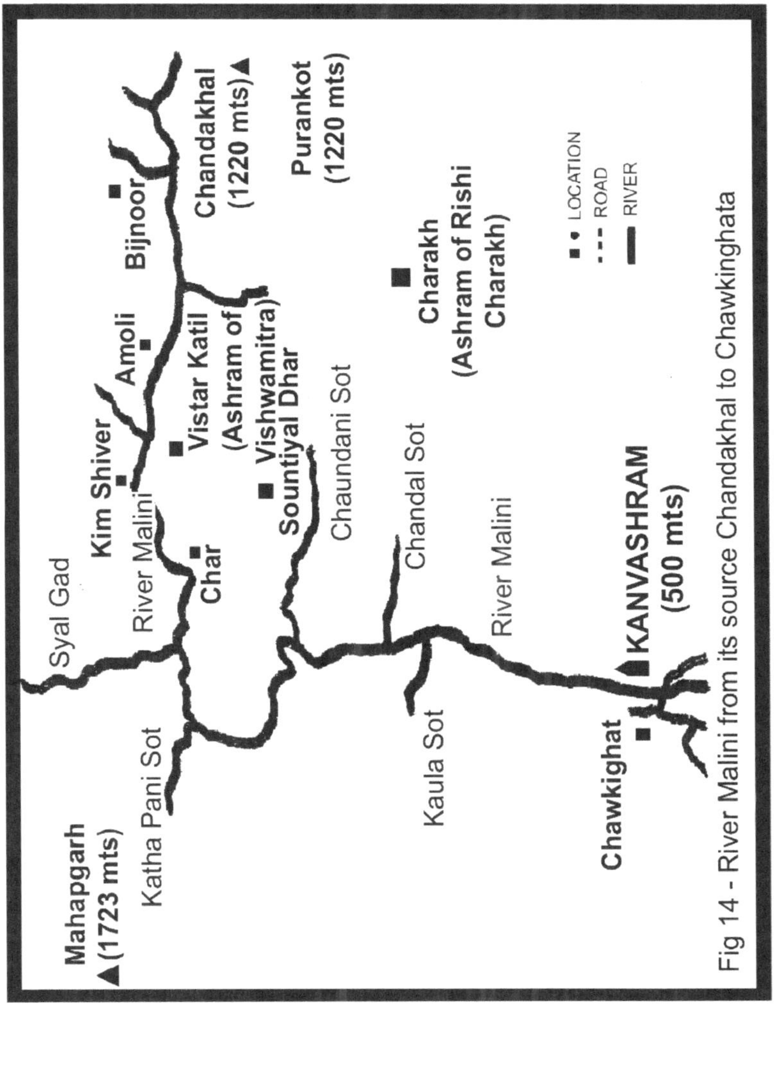

Fig 14 - River Malini from its source Chandakhal to Chawkinghata

river emerges, lies at the East end of the Malini valley, at the base of a prominent hillock called Purankot **(पुराणकोट). (Figure 14)** The trickle of water which emerges from the hillside, flows for about a hundred metres and disappears underground. The water reemerges again about 2 km downstream. A number of other small streams flowing down from, in between the folds of the mountain in the valley, join this mainstream. Most of these streams carry water in them during the rainy season from July to October but go dry thereafter. From its origin in Chandakhal, the river Malini flows westwards.

After travelling 8 km and flowing past Mandai, Saur, Amoli villages, the river makes a 90-degree loop to the South. It flows past Simalna Talla and Malla and other small villages, mostly located on the hilly slopes of the valley. The river further traverses about 10 km, flowing through huge rock boulders and extremely narrow gorges, before emerging onto the plain region at Chawkighat. This small hamlet is situated on the right bank of the river. Right opposite on a raised ground on the left bank is located the symbolic memorial of Kanvashram, built by the government of Uttar Pradesh and the Government of India in 1956 (The Cover Photo of the book).

Not long ago, Chawkighat was a major trading centre of the region. It catered to the basic needs of the inhabitants of the villages in the hills and was connected by a mule

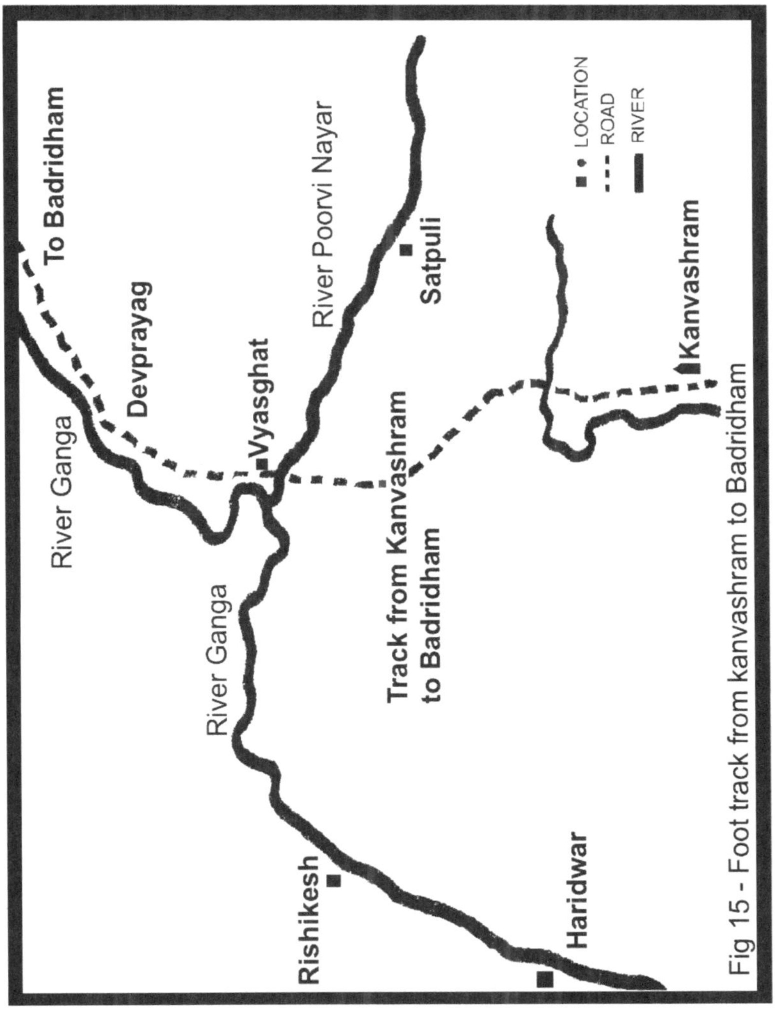

Fig 15 - Foot track from kanvashram to Badridham

track, which ran parallel to the river. The track leading to the villages, proceeded further towards the north direction, onto the bank of river Ganga, meeting it at Vyas ghat in Devprayag. From there on, they merge with other foot tracks, which proceed and terminate at the holy shrine of Badridham and Kedardham. (**Figure 15**) The movement of pilgrims and settlers along the route from Kanvashram to Badridham is evident from the presence and names of several villages established along this path. These settlements were founded by migrants from regions such as Rajputana, Gujarat, and Central India—individuals who may have initially undertaken a pilgrimage but later relocated permanently, likely due to the atrocities inflicted by Muslim invaders during the 16th or 17th centuries. The names of these villages often reflect the migrants' places of origin. For example, my ancestral village, situated near this historic route, is known as Mohini Rawat and lies in Ajmer Patti. *Patti* being a Hindi term denoting a region or strip of land. The name Ajmer indicates the village's historical connection to Ajmer, a prominent city in Rajasthan. Similarly, the adjacent villages are in Udaipur Patti, echoing the name of another significant city from the same state.

Till 1998 the mule track along the river Malini, was maintained by District Council, Pauri Garhwal. Presently, these tracks are in a dilapidated state due to inadequate maintenance and limited movement of villagers. The construction of motorable roads has provided alternate and speedier modes of transportation. The ancient transportation channels that had existed since time immemorial, which originated from Kanvashram and terminated in the holiest shrines of the Hindus, have gradually disappeared into the folds of the forest, through which they pass.

River Malini has witnessed many upheavals and transformations in the region, including the rise and fall of Vedic culture and Kanvashram. However, no significant change seems to have taken place in the path of the river in the hilly region, though its path in the plain region has undergone change. An incident still fresh in the memory of the local inhabitants of the region occurred in Sep 1924. Malini valley and the region around it received incessant continuous heavy downpours for 7 days. The deluge of water which flowed down caused devastating floods in the region. The overflowing river engulfed its banks and destroyed everything in its path. Most of the shops and storage facilities of traders in Chawkighat, were swept away by this torrent of water. There is a possibility that the path of the river was blocked in the narrow valley through which it flows, due to a landslide, which occurs quite frequently in Uttarakhand, as the mountain ranges are very fragile. The water body formed due to such a landslide and its subsequent rupture released a huge quantity of water which destroyed everything in its path. Chawkighat could not recover from this catastrophic destruction. Alternate routes to Badridham came up via Haridwar. These twin tragedies sounded a death knell to the famous trading centre. Today Chawkighat appears desolate, far from its original glorious days, dotted with some thatched huts and some poorly constructed brick houses. The demise of the trading centre ended whatever remained of the fading memory of Kanvashram.

The flow of the river slows down as it enters the plain region at Chawkighat. Its bed widens, as it moves downstream and the river splits into two streams. A small branch of the river moves slightly westwards flowing close to a tri-junction of roads which was called Kalalghati but now addressed as Kanvghati. Both the streams thereafter run somewhat parallel for some distance. Their gap gradually widens as they flow southwards. The smaller westward branch flows past the village Chaturwala about 8 km downstream from Chawkighat. This offshoot of river Malini is called river Ratnal and has limited flow and dries out by the end of the monsoon season in October. It rejoins Malini about 20 km downstream close to town of Najibabad. With incessant illegal mining of the river bed for rocks, sand and gravel for construction, the river bed has gone down considerably. The illegal excavation of material from the river bed has been responsible for the collapse of the bridge constructed across the river Malini, in between Village Haldukhata and Motadakh, in Aug 2023.

The catchment area of the Malini in the mountain region is extremely large, due to which when it rains, huge deluge of water cascades down the hillsides, into the river. The rainwater mixed with the rich virgin soil of the mountain makes the river water reddish-brown, like very strong brewed tea. The agricultural fields irrigated with this rich mineral-laden muddy water, have been rejuvenating the soil of the region and have maintained good agricultural produce. The region irrigated by the water of Malini is and was famous for its high-quality fine basmati rice grown in the region, called *Hansraj*. With time though, there has been a reduction in the total cropped area. There are many reasons for the same. Splitting of land between relatives has resulted in smaller holdings, which have become unsuitable for agriculture. Increase in population has led to land being used for the construction of houses. Further low availability of labour and general trend to shy away from physical work has resulted in a reduction in agriculture output. Changes in climatic conditions and rainfall patterns all over the world, the availability of water in river Malini has also reduced. The river still has water in its bed till Chawkighat even in the hottest months of May and June. Water is tapped for irrigation from the river about one kilometre upstream of Chawkighat. Till 2005, the river water was pumped from the same spot for drinking purposes also. River water which reaches up to Chawkighat, disappears underground and resurfaces further downstream in the dry months. The only town on Malini bank is Najibabad, which is located about 20 km downstream from Chawkighat on its left bank. After travelling about 80 km from its origin in Chandakhal, river Malini merges into the Ganga near a place called Rawali in Uttar Pradesh. **(Figure 16**) Number of villages like Harayapur, Lakhakhurad, Lalpur, Dharampur, Bhoj, Mahaswar etc., are located on its banks. The flow of the river is appreciably low at Rawali.

The name Malini of the river has come about due to the plentiful presence of a creeper called *Malu* or *Malan* growing in abundance in the valley of the river. It was used by the local inhabitants of this region, for various purposes. The creeper has broad leaves, large enough to be used as a plate, to eat food. Two or three leaves were joined by small twigs to make a plate. Food was served on these plates, on all ceremonial occasions like marriage, in religious festivals at home or in temples. Due to abnormal strength, its stem was used as a rope. The plant has medicinal properties and was used in the Ayurveda system of medicine prevalent in the region. Presently, due to changes in the living system, old traditions have been shelved and the use of creeper is confined to some odd individuals who have knowledge of it. The creeper blossoms in summer with a white flower.

The reason the ancestors of rishi Kanv decided to settle on its banks was based on the nature of the river, the environment of the region, weather, safety and security, ease in carrying out agriculture and availability of water. The water of river Malini was and is still pure, refreshing

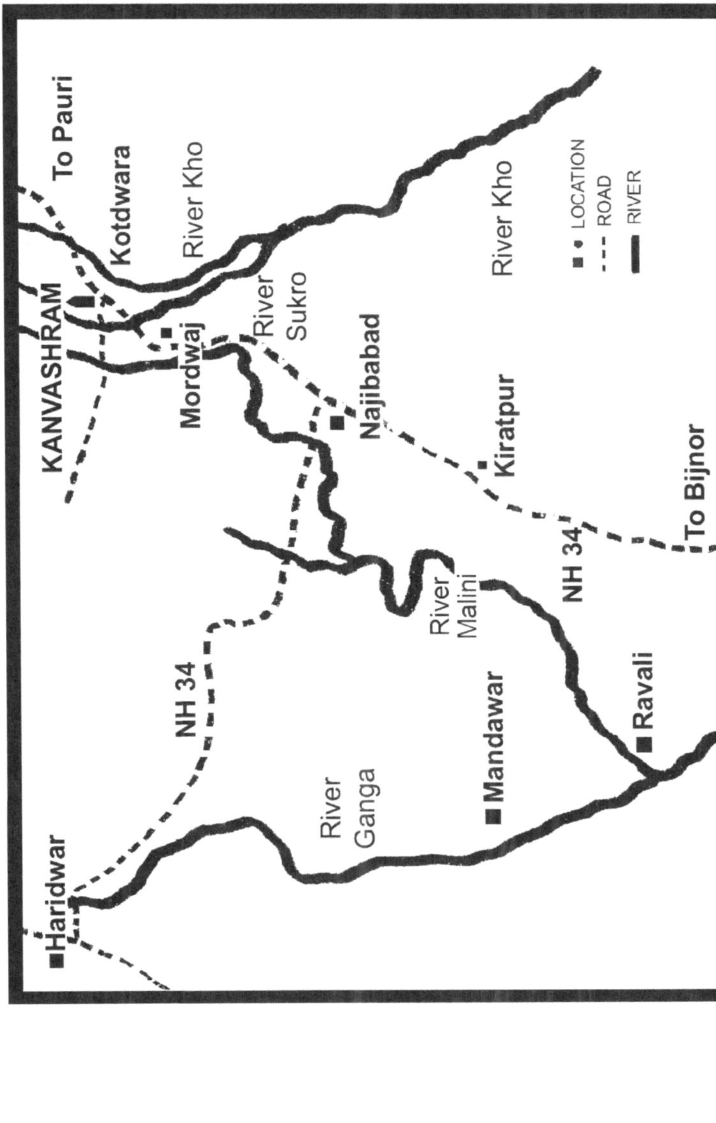

Fig 16 - Path of River Malini from Chawkighata to Ravali

and sweet in taste, unlike water from other sources. With a PH of approximately 7.5 and TDS 384, it is ideal to drink and for cooking. Substantial minerals are present in it but the water of the river is soft. Like other rivers which flow in the region, Malini does not dry out completely even in the hottest months, prior to the monsoon. The presence of dissolved calcium, though substantially low, in the water of the river indicates that the water being released into the river has been trapped in calcium deposits of the mountain range. Shivalik mountain range has large calcium deposits. Extensive mining was done in these mountains, to extract calcium ore but has been stopped since 1990.

Moderate weather conditions exist in the region, more so around Kanvashram, still as on date. The average temperature varies from 35 degree Celsius in summer to about 10 degree Celsius in winter. Kanvashram region through which river Malini flows is still surrounded by forest from three sides. The place is unaffected by storms which rage in the plain region, in the summer months. Continuous light breeze flows in the valley, which keeps the region cool, even during the hottest months of May and June. Sufficient flat land existed adjacent to the foothills close to the ashram which must have been used for agriculture. Besides all the above, the primary factor considered by settlers in choosing a river was driven by the fact that the river's strength should not be dependent on its tributaries. Secondly, it should not be a glacier-fed river.

As these were the two primary factors which contributed to the disappearance of river Sarasvati and the memory of the same was still fresh in the minds of the settlers. Desertion by Sutlej and Jamuna, two main tributaries, was a major blow to river Sarasvati. The second cause was the reduction in the flow of the meltwater, which it received from the glaciers, due to the ending of the warming phase. The third, additional reason was the prolonged weak monsoon in the region. All three factors combined, contributed to the reduction of the flow of Sarasvati and its ultimate disappearance. The settlers were suspicious of the glacier-fed river, as they were uncertain about their continuous future existence. They therefore ruled out the two major glacier-fed rivers Ganga and Jamuna flowing in the region. On the other hand, river Malini was an independent river, not fed by any tributaries. Secondly, its origin was not from a glacier which must also have been observed by the settlers. Besides, Malini had continued availability of water in the hot months of summer, even in case of deficient monsoon. Having met all the required conditions, the ancestors of rishi Kanv after due consideration must have decided to settle on its bank.

Contribution of Malini in the history of this nation, in establishing the ancient Vedic culture, in this subcontinent, is as significant as the position of various *rishis* and other iconic personalities who created the Vedic culture in Kanvashram. Though none of those who once dwelled on her banks are present today, river Malini still gently flows down from the folds of Shivalik mountain ranges, confirming the existence of Kanvashram and reminding all, of the presence of the great centre of education that existed on its banks.

CHAPTER 5

LEGEND

Events and happenings in Kanvashram about the birth of Emperor Bharat and his accession as king have been presented with a slight variation in Mahabharat and Abhigyan Shakuntalam. Poet and dramatist Kalidas has added some events in the drama, to make his creation engrossing and captivating.

Besides describing all the events leading to the great war, the epic is loaded with innumerable stories and narration of various events that happened during a millennium. Complete epic is a maze of stories within a story, recited by various storytellers, at different places and times. Amongst the innumerable stories narrated by storytellers, enumerated in Mahabharat, lies hidden somewhere in the web, is the story of Shakuntala, wife of King Dushyant and mother of Emperor Bharat. When asked by Janmejaya (great-grandson of Arjun) about the origin of Kuru lineage, Vaishampayan, the *suti* or story narrator, starts instead from Bharat lineage. Choosing his words in a systematic manner he describes the events of the past, which occurred about 16 generations before the birth of Pandav and Kauravas. Vaishampayan starts his narration by saying that once upon a time there was a mighty and fearless King Dushyant. The king abided by his *dharma* and was extremely popular with his subject. The people in his kingdom were happy, who lived a comfortable and secure life. Hunting has always been one of the favourite pastime of the kings. One day king Dushyant decides to go out into the jungle on a hunt. The king is accompanied by his entourage and soldiers. As described in Mahabharat, king Dushyant and his soldiers kill numerous animals in the dense jungle. While chasing an injured deer Dushyant emerges from the jungle and finds himself in an open area with a river flowing nearby. He is surprised and amazed to find the place full of flowers, trees laden with fruits. Unable to continue in the chariot, he dismounts from it. There he encounters some holy men collecting dry wood lying on the bank of the river. When asked, they tell him that up ahead is the ashram of *rishi* Kanv. Curious to know more about the *ashram* and *rishi* Kanv, King Dushyant, leaves his soldiers outside to stand guard and enters the *ashram*. In the *ashram,* the king is welcomed by an extremely charming young maiden. She cordially welcomes him into the *ashram* and tells him that her father *rishi* Kanv is presently not in the *ashram*. Surprised at her words, Dushyant asks how she can be the daughter of *rishi* Kanav, as *rishi* Kanv is unmarried. Shakuntala then narrates to the king, what has been told to her, by her father *rishi* Kanv.

Lord Indra, perturbed by the deep meditation of sage Vishvamitra, plans to disturb his meditation. He therefore sends *apsra* Menka from heaven to earth. Menka comes to earth and succeeds in distracting *rishi* Vishvamitra. With their union; a girl child is born to Menka. Having achieved her aim, Menka leaves the child in the jungle, on the bank of river Malini and returns to her heavenly abode. Sage Kanv passing through the jungle is attracted by the loud chirping of birds. On investigating he finds a girl child, surrounded by birds. He takes the child with him to his ashram and brings her up under his care. Shakuntala thereafter says that there are three types of people who can be addressed as a father. One who gives part of his body for the birth of a child. The second person who can be addressed as father is one who protects. Thirdly, a person can be called a father, who feeds. As sage Kanv has protected and fed me since birth, hence he is my father. Deeply impressed by the words and mannerisms, he was also captivated by her beauty and asked her to marry him. Shakuntala requests Dushyant to await the arrival of her father. Dushyant however insists on a *Gandharv* marriage. Reluctantly Shakuntala agrees but extracts a promise from Dushyant, that the child born out of their union, will be the successor to his throne. Dushyant, bitten by the desire to possess Shakuntala, agrees. With the rites of a *gandharv* marriage they unite. He gives Shakuntala his royal ring as a present. Having spent some time in the ashram, Dushyant departs. He promises Shakuntala that he will send his mighty army to escort her to his capital at the earliest. This does not happen as Dushyant forgets the encounter. *Rishi* Kanv on return to the ashram understands the complete situation and tells Shakuntala that she has done no wrong as *gandharv* marriage is superior to all types of marriage as per *dharma*.

Description of the events from this juncture onward, differ in Mahabharat and Abhigyan Shakuntalam, till the meeting and acceptance of Shakuntala and her child by Dushyant. According to Mahabharat, Dushyant leaves the *ashram* after promising Shakuntala that he will return to take her to his kingdom. In due course, Shakuntala gives birth to a boy child. The child grows up in the *ashram* of Kanv and displays qualities of a prince. He plays fearlessly with ferocious wild animals of the jungle like lions and tigers. He is named *Sarvadaman* (one who dominates all) by the inmates of the ashram. One day *rishi* Kanv tells Shakuntala that the child is now old enough to be united with his father Dushyant and be declared prince. Shakuntala thereafter leaves the ashram of Kanv with her son, accompanied by some inmates of the *ashram* and heads to the capital of the kingdom of king Dushyant. They travelled on foot as there is no reference of them crossing a river. Shakuntala appears in the court of Dushyant and tells the king that the child with her is his son. King Dushyant refuses to recognize Shakuntala. She pleads, but Dushyant is unmoved. Shakuntala, thereafter starts to leave his court but at that instant a voice from heaven says "Dushyant you are making a great mistake, this woman is your wife and the boy with her is your son, to be the future king of this nation." Dushyant thereafter tells all his court retinue that he knew all along that Shakuntala was his wedded wife but due to fear of society, he was afraid of accepting her. He thereafter accepts Shakuntala as his Queen and declares the child as prince, to be the future king and his successor.

The most charismatic and captivating narration of the events is written by Kalidas in his creation Abhigyan Shakuntalam. Kalidas can be considered as one of the greatest writers, poets and dramatists of this nation and of the world. His creation Abhigyan Shakuntalam, has been translated into many languages and the drama enacted on stage in countries all over the world. An unparalleled achievement by any standard, Kalidas presented a lively vivid description of Kanvashram and its surrounding region in his creation. With his brilliant writing and description, he has made Kanvashram and all personalities connected with it, Shakuntala, King Dushyant, *rishi* Kanav, *rishi* Vishvamitra, Bharat etc. immortal. A vast number of important events and people simply disappear from history and are not known to future generations. One of the major reasons being that they fail to attract the attention of some great writer, to glorify them and portray the happening of their lifetime events, in his writing. Kanvashram and all associated with it could have been confined to a similar fate, had not Kalidas taken them into his folds and created his master piece Abhigyan Shakuntalam.

From the detailed description of Kanvashram and its surroundings enumerated in the drama, it is evident that Kalidas was familiar with the location of Kanvashram. Kalidas's genius and brilliance were apparent to all since his birth but to undermine his personality, character and image, considerable effort was made by many, by spreading false and fictitious stories about his character and behaviour. One often heard incident narrated about Kalidas is that, while sitting on a branch of a tree he was cutting the base of the branch with an axe, which connected it to the tree. However, these silly stories and gimmicks, which some think as real, did not affect him and his writing. He went on to create many literary masterpieces like Kumarsambhav, Raghuvansham, Megadut, Ritusambhar, Malavi Kaganimitrai etc. The shadow of the terrain, rivers and mountains of Uttarakhand, are seen in his writing and clearly show the influence on him, of his place of birth. In Abhigyan Shakuntalam, the poet creates a series of tragic events which befall Shakuntala before she confronts Dushyant again. Kalidas describes that after spending some time in the ashram Dushyant bids farewell to Shakuntala. He gives her his royal ring as a gift, promising to return and take her to his capital. Saddened by the departure of Dushyant, Shakuntala thereafter remains immersed in his thoughts. She fails to welcome *rishi* Durvasha who comes to the ashram to meet *rishi* Kanv. Enraged, Durvasha curses

Shakuntala, that lost in whose thought she has not given him a befitting welcome, will forget her. The inhabitants of the ashram are extremely disturbed and shocked, when they hear of the curse. They implore Durvasha to forget and forgive. They assure him that Shakuntala regrets the omission and has accepted her mistake. He thereafter says that the curse cannot be revoked but its effect can be reduced. He thereafter says that, when Shakuntala will show something to that person, he will recollect his past memory and remember her. Shakuntala is happy, for she had the king's royal ring with her and was sure that the Dushyant would remember her when she shows the royal ring to him. In due course of time, Shakuntala gives birth to a boy child. The boy grows up in the ashram under the overall care of *rishi* Kanv. One day on the advice of *rishi* Kanv, Shakuntala along with her son and some members of the ashram starts a journey to meet king Dushyant in his capital. The entourage of Shakuntala must have travelled on foot to reach the river Ganga. As described, further journey by the entourage was done on a boat. This was possibly added by Kalidas to create ground for the most tragic episode of the story. The capital of king Dushyant was located to the East of the river Ganga. This is so, as there is no reference of King Dushyant crossing any river either in Mahabharat or Abhigyan Shakuntalam, when he went on a hunt on a chariot and reached Kanvashram. **(Figure 17)** Further, there is a false perception amongst most as they consider Hastinapur as the capital of King Dushyant. It was

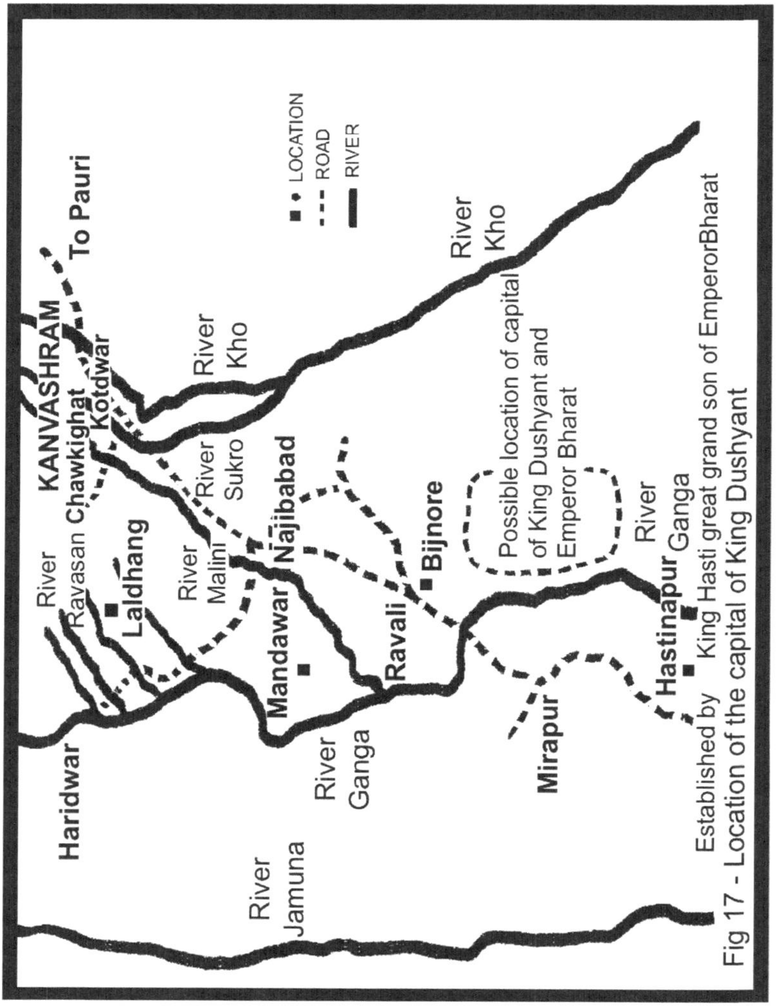

Fig 17 - Location of the capital of King Dushyant

in fact his great-grandson Hasti, who established a new city, West of river Ganga and named it Hastinapur. The city still exists and lies west of river Ganga and was the capital of Pandav and Kaurav.

While journeying on the boat, the royal ring given by Dushyant, slips from Shakuntala's finger, when she dips her hand in the river water. Despite the loss of the royal ring, Shakuntala still presents herself in the court of Dushyant, confident that she will be recognized by the king. Without the ring to remind the king, the curse of Durvasa remains. Dushyant refuses to recognize Shakuntala. She pleads, but Dushyant is unmoved. Shakuntala, thereafter leaves his court and returns to Kanvashram. It seems that the story has come to an end at this juncture but Kalidas brings his imaginative and creative thinking into his writing. What happens next, as described, is nothing short of a miracle. Fortunately, a fisherman while cutting open the fish, he has netted, finds a royal ring in its stomach. While the fisherman was discussing the issue of the ring with his other fellow mates, the conversation was overheard by the king's soldiers. The soldiers arrest the fisherman and produce him in the court of king Dushyant. On seeing the ring Dushyant recollects all and is full of remorse. He gives gifts to the fisherman and the soldiers, much to their dismay, and sets off for Kanvashram, as the effect of the curse of Durvasha was over. On entering Kanvashram he sees a child playing with ferocious lion, whose mouth was opened by him, to count his teeth. On enquiring, the boy tells him that he is the son of Shakuntala. Dushyant thereafter accepts Shakuntala as his Queen and declares the child as prince, to be the future king and his successor. Abhigyan Shakuntalam was translated into English by Wilson Jones in the year 1789.

CHAPTER 6

DESTRUCTION OF KANVASHRAM

History of the world endorses the fact that no civilization, nation or city has continued to remain in existence indefinitely. Some civilisations decline abruptly and vanish without a trace. Others last for thousands of years and many disappear in mere few hundred years. The oldest, largest and longest existing civilisation of the world, Sarasvati-Sindhu civilisation formed over a period, flourished and perished. It rose to the pinnacle of its glory and disappeared leaving traces of its existence, scattered all over the Indian subcontinent. Unlike other civilizations, the Sarasvati-Sindhu civilisation remained in existence for more than 10,000 years. No one can foretell when a civilisation at its peak today may disintegrate. The reasons for the decay of a civilisation can be numerous. Vedic culture which blossomed in the valley of the river Malini, culminated in creation of the first Vedic education system in Kanvashram. It had a wonderful beginning and achieved innumerable highs in education, cultural and spiritual fields. The oldest ancient scripture Rig Veda was composed there. The Vedic education system continued unabated for hundreds of years and was prevalent during the period of the great war of Mahabharat and even afterwards.

Kanvashram remained at the peak of its glory for hundreds of years. It is said that time and tide wait for none. The prominence of Kanvashram as an educational and spiritual centre gradually diminished over time. Vedic culture stipulated a set way of living, in which *yagya*, rituals and sacrifices were considered as the only way to connect to the Gods. It was emphasized that by performing sacrifices and rituals, the Gods would be pleased and in turn bless and protect them. Vedic culture underwent change in the later part of the Vedic age 700–500 BCE. Elaborate ceremonies were required to be performed by common man to please the gods, they were assured that this would in turn protect and bring prosperity to them, their families and clan. Many new texts were written to amplify the rituals and ceremonies. The new rituals introduced were rigidly implemented. The changes introduced were not well received. The interest of the masses in religious rituals gradually declined. Emergence of a new religious sect Buddhism, at this juncture challenged the prevalent Vedic culture. The support and encouragement given to this new religious sect, by the prevailing ruler, Asoka helped in the spread of this new religious sect and established its roots in this nation. Due to royal support for the new religious sect, the importance of Vedic culture diminished and the new religious order became a dominant force. There was a gradual shift of people to the new religion, which rose on the horizon.

Besides Buddhism, another religious sect Jainism, also came into being and caused further erosion to the Vedic culture. The drift of people to the new religious order also affected places of Vedic education, like Kanvashram. It lost its elite position as the nucleus of education and spiritual centres. Its position altered from being a hub of spiritual and educational centres, to that of a religious heritage site. Subsequently, with further decline of Vedic culture, Kanvashram was transformed into a pilgrimage centre. Despite all the changes, Kanvashram did not lose its prominence. The period in which the foresaid transformation took place, is not scripted in any of the ancient scriptures or historical documents. Pilgrims continued to visit the bank of river Malini, to pay homage to the creator of this nation Bharat and *rishi* Kanv. There is ample evidence on the ground and documents to show that Kanvashram held its importance. Pilgrims continued to travel via Kanvashram, on their way to newly created religious sites, deep in the Himalayan mountains, till early 18th century. From Kanvashram, the travellers tracked along the river Malini and reached a place called *Kim Shivar* in the Malini valley. A place where a person can take shelter and rest is called a *Shivar* or in other words a transit camp. It was here the pilgrims stopped to rest, before commencing their ascend-up into the Himalayan mountains. The next distinct location on this journey was Vyas *ghat,* on the bank of river Ganga, tracking through Paukhal, Silogi, Mandalu, Jakhali Khal etc. *Rishi* Vayas whose reference is found in many ancient scriptures possibly had his *ashram* in the region. The foot track from Vayas *ghat* goes further onwards and up into the hills via the five Prayag, Dev, Rudra, Karan, Nand and Vishnu, to the holy shrine Badri Dham, is still in use. **(Figure 15)**

With passage of time, the situation on ground changed and the importance of Kanvashram declined. The ancient pilgrimage route traversed by innumerable pilgrims, for thousands of years to the most pious and spiritual and religious site of this nation, further lost its importance due construction of metallic roads and introduction of new modes of transportation. Pilgrimage which was earlier undertaken on foot was now being done by car, bus or by helicopter. The newly constructed metallic roads via Haridwar reached the holy sites of Badri Dham, Kedar Dham, Gangotri and Yamunotri. The old pilgrim route through Kanvashram faded from memory and so did the importance of Kanvashram. The mountain tracks on the ground gradually disappeared and were ultimately engulfed by the dense jungle and Kanvashram faded from the memory of the people of this nation.

Most civilisations, cities or settlements establish themselves or come up along the bank of rivers or some important travel route. Creation of new routes and abandoning of old pathways lead to collapse of these settlements. Change in the flow path of the rivers due to unforeseen natural calamities, including tectonic upheavals, is another major cause of disintegration of civilization along river banks. Change in the path of some tributaries of river Sarasvati led to the collapse of Sarasvati-Sindu civilisation which flourished on its banks. Fortunately, though the pilgrimage route via Kanvashram was abandoned but forever gentle flowing river Malini neither disappeared nor changed its course. It still traverses the same path that it did thousands of years ago and reminds us of the vibrant and dynamic educational, cultural and spiritual centre Kanvashram which existed on its bank.

The history of this great and mighty nation has seen many upheavals. Some explicit, in the form of invasion by foreign mercenaries from Greeks or Muslim invaders and other hidden changes in the form of religious unrest within the nation. Kanvashram did not remain untouched when the Vedic system of living was challenged. The heat of the Buddhist uprising against the Vedic culture also affected Kanvashram. A Buddhist centre Mordwaj was established close to the Kanvashram. It lies about 4 km downstream of the river Malini from Kanvashram between Kotdwara, Uttarakhand and Najibabad, UP. **(Figure 01)** The ruins of this Buddhist centre can still be seen. Excavation of the site was done by Kham Superintendent (an official appointed by the colonial rulers) and relics of a Buddhist structure obtained are understood to be stored in a museum in Lucknow, Uttar Pradesh. Some pieces of relics though can still be seen in a temple built in the location. Another major Buddhist centre Mandawar is located about 50 km from Kanvashram and close to river Malini. This place finds mention in the book, The Ancient Geography of India authored by Cunningham.

The destruction and annihilation of the ancient Vedic cultural heritage of this great nation Kanvashram and Bharat Varsh commenced simultaneously. After the initial onslaught, Vedic culture and its spiritual aspect prevalent in this nation did recover but it never reached its former glorious self. The re-emergence of the Vedic culture started at the beginning of the first millennium, as changes were introduced in it. The period saw a gradual reduction in the following of the Buddhist sect in the subcontinent. The followers of the Buddhist sect either reverted back to or migrated out of the subcontinent, to countries surrounding this nation. This resulted in the spread of Buddhism to nations like Afghanistan, Tibet, China, Japan, Sri Lanka etc. Though Vedic culture reemerged to some extent in this subcontinent but was unable to re-establish Kanvashram and take it to its former glory. All the religious turmoil that took place in this subcontinent did not eliminate the Vedic education system, whose fundamental unit was *gurukul.* These gurukuls were supported by major education institutes.

The nation Bharat was in the process of consolidation and recovery from the turmoil lasting a millennium when it faced another setback. The nomads surrounding the subcontinent have been forever attracted by the immense wealth possessed by this nation. The initial encounter with the Arabs invaders took place in the early 8th century. The forces of Mohamad Bin Qasim managed to capture Sindh but were driven back when they tried to move further inwards, into this nation. The invaders were so brutally annihilated, that they did not return, for the next 400 years. After innumerable futile intrusions, they finally penetrated the nation's boundaries and gained entry into this nation in the 12th century. Having lost the first battle of Tarain in 1191, Mohammed Gauri once again returned to challenge the might of the powerful King of Rajputana, Prithavi Raj Chauhan. In 1192, he once again faced Prithvi Raj Chauhan in the same battlefield of Tarain near Thanesar, in present-day Haryana state, about 150 km north of Delhi, with a force composed of thugs and thieves. With deceit, he managed to defeat Prithavi Raj Chauhan. This decisive battle was a turning point in the history of this nation. Foreign invaders finally gained their first foothold in this subcontinent. After establishing their authority around Delhi, the invaders systematically plundered all religious and culturally important sites of this subcontinent. Haridwar and adjacent religious places, which included Kanvashram, were razed to the ground. Further destruction of the region was done in 1227 by the forces of Iltumush, which attacked the Mandawar and Bijnor region.

The destruction of Kanvashram, which started with the advent of the Muslim raiders in the 12th century, finally ended in completely erasing the very existence of the world-famous educational centre, from the face of the earth. Nothing remained in the region except the jungles, which gradually became denser by the day and the gently flowing river Malini. In the 19th century after defeating the Gorkhas of Nepal, the British colonial rulers of this nation split the Garhwal region, in present-day Uttarakhand, in two parts. The area, North of river Ganga was given to the King of Garhwal and the region south of the river, in which Kanvashram was located, came under colonial rule. Jim Corbett came as a hunter to this region but dedicated his life to protecting the people of the Garhwal and Kumaon region by eliminating the ferocious man-eaters, which prowled in these jungles. The British came to hunt animals but the thugs and dacoits residing in these dense jungles were a deterrent to those wishing to settle in Kotdwara or its surrounding region near Kanvashram. The area was the domain of dacoit Sultana. He was finally apprehended in 1923 from the jungles of Najibabad or someplace close to Nainital. A trial was held in court under the name 'Nainital Gun Case'. Jim Corbet in his book Young India has written that Sultana was like Robinhood, who never looted the poor but helped them. It was only after his death that people began to settle in this region. New village settlements were established, by the colonial rulers, to increase food productivity, in this fertile region, fed by river Malini. With the gradual increase in population, Kanvashram once again started to emerge on the map of this nation Bharat.

CHAPTER 7

RE-EMERGENCE

Kanvashram never really emerged back to its former glory. After this nation gained independence in 1947, a faint light appeared at the end of the tunnel but it soon faded away. Post-independence, demand for reconstruction of Somnath temple, one of the most revered religious sites of this nation, destroyed and plundered a number of times by invaders, was voiced by people of this newly independent nation but the government paid no heed to their repeated request. Nehru, the self-appointed Prime minister of the nation, was against the reconstruction of destroyed ancient Hindu religious monuments and was a constant source of hindrance, in any effort undertaken in this direction. However, in the case of Somnath temple, with effort of people of Gujrat and active support of Dy Prime Minister of India, Iron Man of this nation, Sardar Vallabhbhai Patel, the temple was rebuilt but further no other Hindu religious site could be reconstructed in the newly independent nation. Nehru tried his utmost to prevent and even threatened, the then President of India, Dr. Rajendra Prasad, not to inaugurate the newly constructed Somnath temple complex. Despite threats and intimidation by Nehru, Dr. Rajendra Prasad went ahead and inaugurated the Somnath temple in May 1951.

Kanvashram and many other major Hindu religious sites like the temple of Lord Ram in Ayodhya, Lord Krishna in Mathura, Kashi etc., destroyed by invaders, were never considered for reconstruction and glorification. A story has been going around for a long time that it was Nehru, who was responsible for the construction of the Kanvashram memorial post-independence at Chawkighat, in 1956. As per the saying, Nehru visited the USSR, (now Russia) in 1955. During his visit, a ballet composed on the drama Abhigyan Shakuntalam, written by Kalidas, was shown to him. After the performance, reporters asked Nehru where Kanvashram was located. Having no knowledge about the ancient heritage of this nation, he had no answer. The fact about the visit of Nehru has been confirmed by the Embassy of India, Moscow Russia via the Ministry of External Affairs, India. He did visit the USSR in 1955. However, the event about the presentation of the ballet was not confirmed. The story continues, that on his return Nehru deputed Shri Sampurna Nand, CM of Uttar Pradesh to locate the historical heritage site. The CM of UP did visit Chawkighat, Kotdwara in Nov 1955 and this fact is confirmed by L. P. Nathani in his book Malini ka Khandar. Chief minister during his visit declared that a memorial would be erected on the bank of river Malini indicating the symbolic presence of Kanvashram.

The twist in the story is that though CM of UP did come to Chawkighat but not on instruction of Nehru, as the story connected with Nehru is fabricated, false and untrue, based on the simple fact that the drama Abhigyan Shakuntalam was converted into a ballet and presented to the people of Russia by composer Sergey Balasanian, in 1963 in the town of Riga in Russia. Nehru had visited Russia in 1955. The story about initiating the glorification of Kanvashram by Nehru also cannot be true, as Nehru was against the reconstruction and glorification of any Hindu religious site. Further, a well-thought-out conspiracy was hatched by Nehru to distort the history of this nation. Corrupted and falsified history of this nation was prepared and presented through various textbooks, introduced in schools and colleges. The task of distorting the history of this nation was achieved with the active support of six successive Union Ministers of Education, appointed by Nehru during his tenure from 1947 to 1964, all of whom were Muslim. They ensured that the true history of this nation remains buried under and inaccurate and misleading history taught to the students of this nation. They were unaware of the fact that truth has a way of emerging, no matter how long it is suppressed or how deep it is buried.

On the other hand, there were many who were working selflessly during that period, to unearth the true history of this nation. An unknown and unheard ordinary citizen of this newly independent nation was working silently and tirelessly, to locate Kanvashram and uncover its historical past. The person who factually brought the existence of Kanvashram in the 20th century was Shrinidhi Sidhantalankar. Unfortunately, he never got any credit for the same. He was born in 1897, in a small village close to Narwar Garh, Madhya Pradesh. As per the introduction given about him by Dr. D. Kalada, in his book *Malini Ke Vano Me*, he was born into an ordinary family. Following the age-old tradition, his parents sent him to a *gurukul* in Haridwar, Uttarakhand at the tender age of 5 years for education. How his desire and passion for the ancient heritage site Kanvashram was kindled is not clear in his books. It is possible that during his education in *gurukul*, he must have studied various epics like Mahabharata, Puranas, etc. These ancient documents must have provided him with the basic information and given him sufficient incentive, to know more about the place, described there and compelled him to go in search, to locate the ancient heritage site. It was fortunate for him as Kanvashram happened to lie about ~30 miles (50 km) south-south-east of Haridwar, where he grew up and received his education. Despite limited information available, he pressed on and tracked the 80 km long stretch of river Malini, in search of Kanvashram. He was a keen hunter and shooter but with a difference. He used his camera to capture the environment and its occupants. For defence against wild animals, he was armed with a bow and arrows. In the early 20th century, an ordinary man of this nation, armed with a bow and arrow to defend himself and a camera to capture the vibrant moments, traversed through the dense jungles surrounding river Malini, teaming with wild animals, to locate the ancient heritage site Kanvashram.

On four different occasions, he traversed the complete region around and along the river Malini, from its source to the place where Malini merges into river Ganga. He carefully documented and scripted his adventurous experience in his books. His first book *Shivalik Ki Ghatio Me* was published and released to the public in August 1955. Based on the authentic research done by Srinidhi Sidhantalankar on Kanvashram, the government of Uttar Pradesh, in consultation with other scholars went ahead and erected a symbolic memorial of Kanvashram, on the left banks of river Malini at Chawkighat, Kotdwara, Dist-Pauri Garhwal. The foundation of the memorial, to honour *rishi* Kanv and Emperor Bharat was laid by Shri Jagmohan Singh Negi, Forest Minister, Uttar Pradesh government, who was the Member of the Legislative Assembly (MLA) from this region, in 1956, on *Basant Panchami* day. Five marble statues, of *rishi* Kanv, *rishi* Kashyap, King Dushyant, Shakuntala and Bharat, playing with a lion were placed in the memorial.

A marble plaque affixed on the wall of the monument, **(Figure 18)** at the time of the inauguration of the memorial, has verses engraved in Sanskrit, which hails the people of this nation,

"मनसि यदि तव स्याज्जन्मना गर्वलेशो ।
भरतभुवि रतिश्च प्रक्तनायाँ समृद्धौ ।।
विरम सुजन किस्चित्पुण्य कण्वाश्रमेश्स्मिधा ।
न्स्मर च भरत पितरों मालिनीकूलकेली: ।।
तमोंग्रस्तस्य विश्वस्य लोक रश्मि प्रदर्शका: ।
वयमेव पुरश्भूम भूयस्तद्वम्दवामहे ।।
पशुरेव न जानीयादात्मनोश्तीत गौरवम् ।
न यथा पश्व: स्यामस्तथा शश्वविद्यातातमहे ।।
लोकस्य द्वेषमात्सय विग्रहाक्षित्पचेतस: ।
विश्व मैत्री प्रतिष्ठायै पंचशीले श्मामहे ।।"

"For if you have the slightest pride in yourself for having taken birth in this ancient prosperous land of Bharat. O' gentle human, stop for a while on the banks of the river Malini at Kanvashram and remember the ancestors of Bharat. For it is them, who have given the ray of light of knowledge, to the people of this world, to drive away the evils of ignorance. We should strive not to become like an animal, who is not proud of his forefathers, as he does not know about the past glory of its ancestors. We should fight to remove from the world, mutual differences, ill will and unpleasantness amongst us by honouring the universal bonds of friendliness and dignity by following the path of Panchsheel".

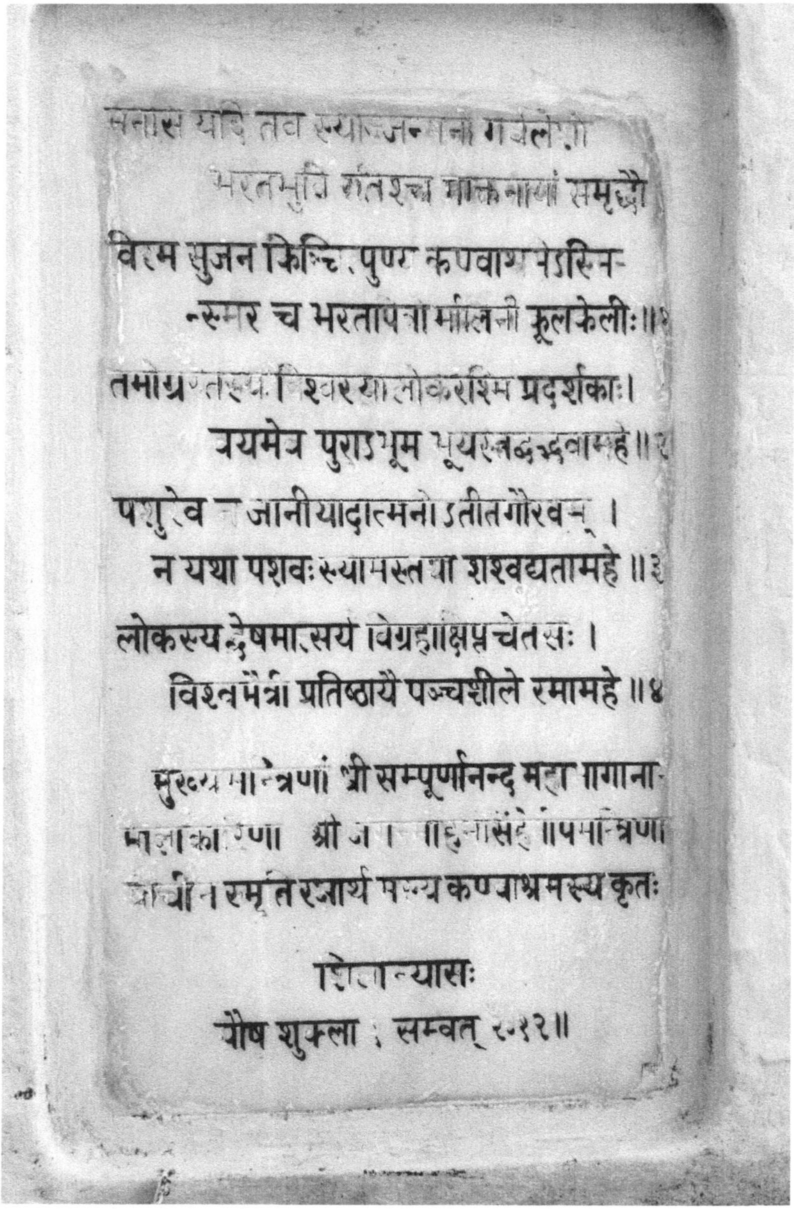

Fig 18 Marble plate

Consequent to the inauguration of the monument, a committee was formed by the residents of the region for the care, maintenance, and upkeep of the monument. It was named Kanvashram Vikas Samiti. The inauguration of the memorial gave rise to a new tradition in this region. A *mela* was thereafter organised every year, on *Basant Panchami,* to celebrate the occasion and pay respect to the ancestors and the creator of this nation. In 1972, 0.364 hectares of land around the monument was given on lease to the Samiti by the Uttar Pradesh government and the Samiti was officially made the caretaker of the memorial. The Samiti besides managing the monument was guided by one basic motto to bring Kanvashram, birthplace of Emperor Bharat back into the national limelight. Though established, no further glorification of the memorial was undertaken by the government of Uttar Pradesh. In 1965, the *Panchami Mela* was given due recognition by the District Council of Pauri Garhwal. Having received official recognition various government departments like animal husbandry, horticulture, family health, agriculture etc., started to take an active part in the *Mela.* They erected stalls to provide information and displayed items related to their department e.g., seeds, medicines for cattle, informative pamphlets on health etc., to villagers which caused a surge in the number of villagers flocking to the Mela. In line with the policies of the government, the Samiti was registered in 1992.

Over the years since independence, a number of eminent persons and academicians of this region have contributed towards spreading information about Kanvashram. Prominent amongst them is Shrinidhi Sidhantalankar. His two books **शिवालिक की घाटियाँ** and **मालिनी के वनो मे** provide information of the region around Kanvashram. Shri Lalita Prasad Nathani was another person, a lawyer by profession, who served as President, Municipal Corporation, Kotdwara for some time. Essay written by him and others on Kanvashram, were compiled by him and presented in the form of two books, **शकुन्तला की मालिनि** (possibly in 1958 or later) and **मालिनि सभ्यता के खण्डर** (1983). Shri Kuwar Singh Negi "*Karmat*" (1909–2012), a centenarian, was a writer, publisher and social worker. His magnanimous contribution cannot be forgotten. He wrote a number of articles on Kanvashram in magazines/newspapers and travelled far and wide to garner support, to bring Kanvashram on the map of this nation. A book in Hindi titled **कण्वाश्रम, चक्रवंती स्रमाठ भरत की जन्म स्थली** authored by me was released on *Basant Panchami* by Honourable Chief Justice of Uttarakhand, Shri Vijai Kumar Bist, on 24 Jan 2015. On 15 May 2016, a website www.kanvashram.org was launched in English, giving detailed information about Kanvashram. Its Hindi translation was uploaded six months later. The English translation of the book titled **Kanvashram- Birth Place of Emperor Bharat** was published later in Nov 2017.

Numerous articles have been written and published by different individuals about Kanvashram in local newspapers and magazines over the years but somehow, they failed to attract the attention of national media and the political leadership of this nation. The primary reason being the hostile political conditions that prevailed in the nation till 2014. The anti-Hindu cultural legacy propagated by Nehru stayed deeply embedded in the policies and working of the government persisted. Things took a turn after Shri Narendra Modi took over the reins of the government as Prime Minister of the nation Bharat Varsh in 2014. A scheme envisioned by the Honourable Prime Minister was launched in 2016 to glorify various ancient heritage sites of this nation. Under the scheme, 100 heritage sites were to be identified in this nation and declared ICONIC, for development and glorification. The first list of such sites was released in 2016 and the second in 2017. The book **कण्वाश्रम, चक्रवर्ती स्रमाठ भरत की जन्म स्थली** written by me, was presented to Member of Parliament from Almora, Uttarakhand, Shri Ajay Tamta, Union Minister of Textile, Govt of India in Feb 2018, as evidence about the presence of ancient heritage site Kanvashram. Further, consultation on the contents of the book was done by the minister with Mr. Mahesh Sharma, Union Minister of Tourism, Government of India. With sufficient information available, Kanvashram was recognized as an ancient heritage site, to be glorified and was included in the 3rd list of 10 Iconic places declared by the Government of India, on 12 June 2018. **(Figure 19)** With official recognition, Kanvashram once again bounced back onto the national portal, from which it has faded and from the memory of the people of this nation. A distinct surge in the search on the web and the people visiting the memorial is an indicator of its re-emergence.

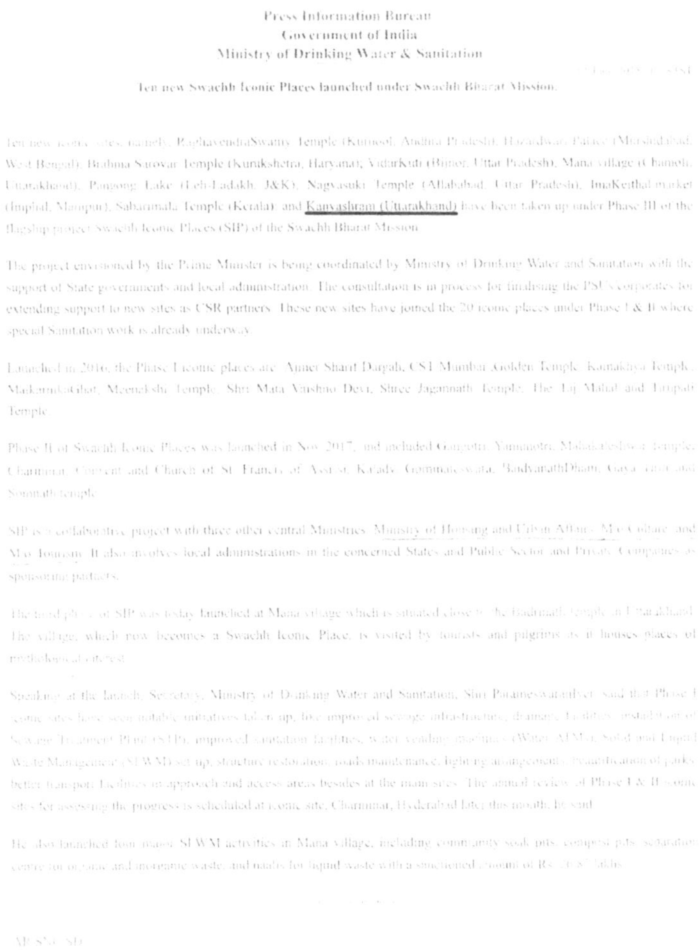

Press Information Bureau
Government of India
Ministry of Drinking Water & Sanitation

[illegible]

Ten new Swachh Iconic Places launched under Swachh Bharat Mission.

Ten new iconic sites, namely, RaghavendraSwamy Temple (Kurnool, Andhra Pradesh), Hazardwari Palace (Murshidabad, West Bengal), Brahma Sarovar Temple (Kurukshetra, Haryana), VidurKuti (Bijnor, Uttar Pradesh), Mana village (Chamoli, Uttarakhand), Pangong Lake (Leh-Ladakh, J&K), Nagvasuki Temple (Allahabad, Uttar Pradesh), ImaKeithal market (Imphal, Manipur), Sabarimala Temple (Kerala) and Kanvashram (Uttarakhand) have been taken up under Phase III of the flagship project Swachh Iconic Places (SIP) of the Swachh Bharat Mission.

The project envisioned by the Prime Minister is being coordinated by Ministry of Drinking Water and Sanitation with the support of State governments and local administration. The consultation is in process for finalising the PSUs/corporates for extending support to new sites as CSR partners. These new sites have joined the 20 iconic places under Phase I & II where special Sanitation work is already underway.

Launched in 2016, the Phase I iconic places are: Ajmer Sharif Dargah, CST Mumbai, Golden Temple, Kamakhya Temple, ManikarnikaGhat, Meenakshi Temple, Shri Mata Vaishno Devi, Shree Jagannath Temple, The Taj Mahal and Tirupati Temple.

Phase II of Swachh Iconic Places was launched in Nov 2017, and included Gangotri, Yamunotri, Mahakaleshwar Temple, Charminar, Convent and Church of St. Francis of Assisi, Kalady, Gommateswara, BaidyanathDham, Gaya Tirth and Somnath temple.

SIP is a collaborative project with three other central Ministries: Ministry of Housing and Urban Affairs, M/o Culture and M/o Tourism. It also involves local administrations in the concerned States and Public Sector and Private Companies as sponsoring partners.

The third phase of SIP was today launched at Mana village which is situated close to the Badrinath Temple in Uttarakhand. The village, which now becomes a Swachh Iconic Place, is visited by tourists and pilgrims as it houses places of mythological interest.

Speaking at the launch, Secretary, Ministry of Drinking Water and Sanitation, Shri ParameswaranIyer, said that Phase I iconic sites have seen notable initiatives taken up, like improved sewage infrastructure, drainage facilities, installation of Sewage Treatment Plant (STP), improved sanitation facilities, water vending machines (Water ATMs), Solid and Liquid Waste Management (SLWM) set up, structure restoration, roads maintenance, lighting arrangements, beautification of parks, better transport facilities in approach and access areas besides at the main sites. The annual review of Phase I & II iconic sites for assessing the progress is scheduled at iconic site, Charminar, Hyderabad later this month, he said.

He also launched four major SLWM activities in Mana village, including community soak pits, compost pits, segregation centre for organic and inorganic waste, and nadis for liquid waste with a sanctioned amount of Rs. [illegible] lakhs.

AP/SNC/SD

Fig 19 Photograph of Iconic Letter

CHAPTER 8

ARCHAEOLOGICAL FIND

It cannot be said with certainty, as to when the first archaeological remains of ancient ruins in Kanvashram region were unearthed. No documented information is available as to when and where the relics were spotted by local inhabitants. However, it is certain that the relics of the ancient structure had surfaced time and again, due to erosion of the surface soil, caused by flowing rainwater, more so in the years, when the monsoon rains were intense in the region. Local inhabitants must have stumbled on them, while moving through the forest in search of herbs, dry wood or on a hunt or while tracking from one village to another. The finely carved stones must have been a source of curiosity. In the course of time, after due deliberation amongst themselves, the inhabitants removed the relics and ceremoniously installed the finely carved pieces, in local temples, as deity stones. All this has happened in the recent past, say about ~100 years ago, when the region was scantily populated. **(Figure 20)** The oldest temples in the area came up about ~80 years ago. It is certain that these relics were unearthed in the year 1924 when the region received extremely heavy rains. In 1956 the Department of Forest,

Uttarakhand, fenced an area of about 12 hectares of land, to create a Deer Park, in the area where the relics are presently being unearthed. The contractor building the wall collected these scattered relic pieces and generously used them in the wall made around the Deer Park, in Chawkighat. These pieces of monuments presently lie safe, cemented in the boundary wall of Deer Park. **(Figure 21)**

The remains of ancient monuments were not restricted to a particular spot but spread over an area measuring about 3 km by 2 km, or maybe more. During the course of my search in the region, I have spotted pieces of relics lying at distant places. **(Figure 07)**. Some not-so-fine pieces have been used by the local villagers in the construction of walls or some other structure, in the temple complex, in the region.

Fig 20 - Relics found in Kanvashram region placed as Deities in temples

Fig 21 - Relic found next to Deer Park are cemented in the wall made around it.

Location, where these relics have been found, lies close to the bank of river Malini, around the hamlet Chawkighat. It is here the river Malini leaves the hilly terrain and enters the plain region. The complete area, where the relics are being found, is referred to in local terminology as *Bhabar* and is defined as a region, which lies at the base of a mountain or foothill. This area presently under consideration is a piece of populated land, about ~3 km wide and ~15 km long which lies along the foothill of Shivalik mountain range and is surrounded by forest from three sides. This land holds a town Kotdwara and about 50-odd villages. Three rivers cut through this region flowing down from the mountain range. The rivers are - to the East Kho, in the middle Sukro and to the West is river Malini. **(Figure 01)** Sukro is a seasonal river that flashes out of the mountain in the monsoon but disappears by the month of October. Its water flows into the river Kho, on whose bank is situated the town of Kotdwara, Uttarakhand.

1991 is recorded as one of those years when Kanvashram region experienced more than average rainfall but something has changed by then. Earlier, the rain water flowing downhill used to discharge into the plain region via various natural shallow channels formed in the sloping land in the region but one of the shallow channels was blocked due construction of the boundary wall of the Deer-park in 1956. The newly constructed boundary wall diverted the flow of water along the boundary wall and created a new channel. This fresh flow path of the rainwater washed away the mud and uncovered remains of ancient relics. The news of the uncovering of the relics spread around. With no electric or electronic communication network in this area in 1991, the news did not travel far. The Kishanpuri telephone exchange about 4 km from Chawkighat came into existence only in 1993. However, news has a way of travelling and reaching the concerned. The presence of these relics reached Garhwal University, Srinagar, Uttarakhand. A team from the University visited the site at Chawkighat. The team after a brief scrutiny carried away with them a few of these pieces, for further investigation and study at the university. Some others were left and can still be found embedded in the front yard of the GMVN tourist Bungalow, located next to Deer Park. In a report submitted by the Garhwal University,

Srinagar to the Archaeological Survey of India, New Delhi the university assessed the age of these relics to be between 10th and 12th century CE. **(Appendix A)** Things thereafter seem to have been laid to rest and no further excavation was carried out by the Garhwal University or Archaeological Survey of India (ASI) in the region.

Exactly two decades later, the situation or circumstances that had occurred due to the ferocity of nature in 1991, in the form of intense rain occurred once again in 2012. Heavy monsoon rainfall further deepened and widened the *nalla* and many relics buried there emerged. However, the situation in 2012 was vastly different from 1991. The news of the presence of the relics reached me as I reside about 2 km from the site. Being the President of Kanvashram Vikas Samiti, an NGO that has been working for the development and recognition of the national heritage site Kanvashram, I along with members of the Samiti visited the site to appraise ourselves of the situation. It was July 2012 and the monsoon was still very active. The site was located about 500 m, from the motorable dirt road in the forest. The entire area was covered in dense vegetation. With effort, the site was located. **(Figure 22)** The relics of some ancient monuments were seen lying scattered in the nalla, which at that instant still had a tickle of water flowing in it. Though pictures of numerous excavated sites have been seen in books and videos, the pleasure and joy of witnessing freshly unearthed relics of some ancient monument with one's naked eyes, is a once in a life event. There are many questions that come up. Where did the structure actually stood? Who constructed them? What did they represent? Did it disintegrate and collapse due to wear and tear or was it brought down by some foreign invaders?

Fig 22 - Members of Kanvashram Vikas samiti inspecting the relics found in September 2012

I had no answer to any of these questions.

Most of the ancient structures are robust and well-built, so there are only two possibilities that might have caused the collapse of these buildings. Either they collapsed due to a landslide in the region, as the place where the relics have been found is located at the base of a hill. The remains could have reached there having been swept down from their original location, due to a landslide or by some other force of nature, possibly an earthquake. The other likelihood is that they were brought down by one of the many invaders who had entered this nation's boundaries since 800 CE. Several baked clay pieces were seen lying scattered about and many were embedded in different layers of now exposed *nalla* side wall. Photographs of the various relics and the site were taken and with a covering note forwarded by me to the Director General, Archaeological Survey of India, New Delhi by email on 25th July 2012. It was a pleasant surprise when I found a reply the very next day in my mailbox, stating that the ASI Circle office, Dehradun, Uttarakhand, is being directed to visit the site at the earliest possible opportunity. The visit to the site was fixed on 23rd September 2012 by ASI Circle office, Dehradun. A team of three archaeologists led by the Superintending Archaeologist, Mr. Atul Bhargava arrived as scheduled. I briefed them about the importance of Kanvashram and its ancient heritage. Several documentary evidence confirming the presence of Kanvashram on the bank of river Malini was also shown to the team. The site is located about 3 km from my residence. **(Figure 23)**

The archaeologist team went about their job and took various photos of the relics on the site and collected pieces of the broken pottery. The team leader Mr. Bhargava, informed the press and those present on the site, that by a rough estimate based on the carving of the relic, that they seem to be from a period anywhere from 800 to 1300 BCE, but the correct or precise dates can only be concluded on further study of the relics, based on their typical built or

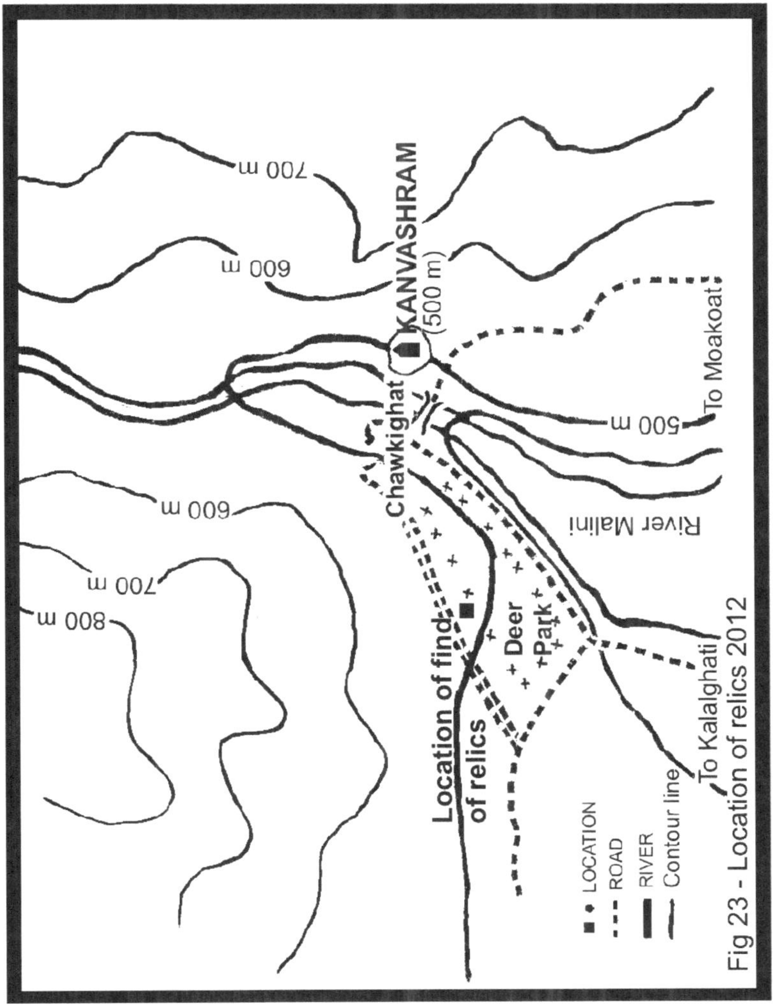

Fig 23 - Location of relics 2012

design. A brief report was prepared by the office of ASI, Dehradun and forwarded to the Director, ASI, New Delhi in Nov 2012. **(Appendix B)** The report concludes that these relics possibly are part of a demolished temple. The relics found seem to form the lowermost level of the structure. By assessing the physical and geographical topography of the area, it is quite likely that the main structure was close to or on high ground towards the hill. Though the place was covered in dense vegetation but with the cooperation of all, it should be possible to locate the main part of the structure. The report recommended that it is necessary to carry out a detailed survey and excavation of the complete area. The report submitted to the HQ ASI, New Delhi by Circle Office Dehradun did not draw any response. Chief Justice Uttarakhand Shri V.K. Bist, who visited the site, sometime in Oct 2012 raised the issue of safety of all the relics with the DFO, Lansdowne range. All the relics unearthed were thereafter removed by the Uttarakhand Forest Department and stored safely in the Deer Park, Chawkighat. Refer DFO, Lansdowne letter 1520(1)/33-7 dated 26th October 2012. **(Figure 24)**

Monsoon rains in the period 2012 to 2015 were normal. As no substantial erosion of land took place in the area, no new relics surfaced, though they could be clearly seen embedded in the soil. In Jan 2016, it came to my knowledge that an extremely fine piece of relic was found and has been removed from the site and stored in a room

Tel/Fax NO 01382-228467
E-mail- dfo_lansdowne@yahoo.com

कार्यालय प्रभागीय वनाधिकारी, लैन्सडौन वन प्रभाग, कोटद्वार।

पत्रांक:– / .दिनांक, कोटद्वार, 26 ,अक्टूबर, 2012.

सदा म

वन क्षेत्राधिकारी,
कोटद्वार।

विषय:– **आरक्षित वन क्षेत्रों में उपलब्ध मूर्तियां।**

श्री वी0के0विष्ट, मा0न्यायाधीश, मा0 उच्च न्यायालय, नैनीताल के द्वारा इस वन प्रभाग के अन्तर्गत स्थान कण्वाश्रम क्षेत्र का भ्रमण किया गया। भ्रमण के दौरान उनके द्वारा कण्वाश्रम क्षेत्र में उपलब्ध मूर्तियों को एक स्थान पर रखने हेतु निर्देशित किया गया है। अतः कण्वाश्रम क्षेत्र के अन्तर्गत जो भी मूर्तिया आपको मिले उनको एक स्थान पर संग्रहालय के रूप में रखने की कार्यवाही की जाय तथा उनक फोटोग्राफ्स ले लिये जाय ताकि भविष्य में इन फोटोग्राफ्सों का अवलोकन मा0 न्यायाधीश को कराया जा सकें।

इसे आवश्यक समझें।

प्रभागीय वनाधिकारी,
लैन्सडौन वन प्रभाग, कोटद्वार।

पत्रांक:– 1520 (1)/33-7 ,दिनांकित।

प्रतिलिपि–उप प्रभागीय वनाधिकारी, कोटद्वार को सूचनार्थ एवं आवश्यक कार्यवाही हेतु प्रेषित।

प्रतिलिपि–कण्वाश्रम मन्दिर([illegible] गुरुकुल महाविद्यालय, कण्वाश्रम, कोटद्वार–गढ़वाल को सूचनार्थ प्रेषित।

प्रभागीय वनाधिकारी,
लैन्सडौन वन प्रभाग, कोटद्वार।

I.C-Camp-2012

Fig 24 – DFO Landsdowne Letter

in the Deer Park by the Forest Department, Uttarakhand. The image of the relic was forwarded to the Director, ASI, New Delhi. **(Figure 25)** A team from ASI, Dehradun office once again came to Kanvashram to investigate and study the relic in question. The team led by Dr. K.C. Nauriyal, Superintending Archaeologist, ASI Circle, Dehradun, visited Kanvashram on 08 February 2016 and studied the various relics unearthed. No copy of the report, if one was submitted to HQ ASI, New Delhi by the Dehradun office of ASI on the subject, was received by Kanvashram Vikas Samiti.

In February 2017, it came to light that all the relics placed under the custody of the Forest Department, Uttarakhand have been removed from the Deer Park, Chawkighat, the place they were stored for viewing by the visitors. Kanvashram Vikas Samiti, taking cognizance of the matter, reported the issue of the disappearance of the relics to the local administration and requested the Forest Department, Uttarakhand, to intimate the whereabouts of the relics. It subsequently came to light that 11 pieces of the finest relics, placed in the safe custody of the Forest Department were discretely handed over by DFO, Forest Department, Lansdowne to a private institution without intimation or approval of the local administration or the ASI, Circle Office, Dehradun. Efforts were initiated by the Samiti to get the relics back as they had by now become a source of attraction and were being viewed by the large number of tourists who came to visit Kanvashram.

Fig 25 - Chamunda relic found in 2015

The matter of illegal removal and handing over of the relics to a private university in Haridwar was brought to the notice of the Forest Department Uttarakhand and the District administration. No action was taken by either, to undo the wrong. The issue was thereafter brought to the notice of the Uttarakhand Government, Cultural Department. Realizing the gravity of the situation, the Cultural Department directed the Gurukul Kangri University, Haridwar to return the relics. All the 11 relics were thereafter returned and handed over to the Samiti. Further, the Cultural Department authorised Kanvashram Vikas Samiti to collect and display all relics found in the Kanvashram region in their Library cum Museum located in Village – Bhim Singh Pur, Kotdwara.

As further excavation in Kanvashram was required, a request for the same was sent to ASI HQ, New Delhi and Circle Office, Dehradun to undertake excavation at the site, based on the report submitted in 2012. A team of archaeologists along with a survey team was deputed from ASI, Lucknow office to visit the site. A team headed by Mrs. Lily Dashmana, Superintending Archaeologist, ASI Circle Dehradun and five other members arrived on 19 Jan 2018, to carry out a survey of the area. A detailed study and survey of the site was carried out. Assistance as required by the team in the form of logistics and manpower was provided by Kanvashram Vikas Samiti to the visiting team, as has been done in the past. A report on the visit was prepared by the

ASI Circle Office, Dehradun and submitted to ASI HQ, New Delhi in Feb 2018 vide their letter No. 2/15/2016-EE/1107 dated 09.02.2018. **(Appendix C)** The report further reiterated all that was stated in the earlier report submitted in 2012 and recommended that a "Trial Trench" excavation be done to uncover the historical remains in the region.

In February 2018 a member of Kanvashram Vikas Samiti, Mr. Praveen Purohit met Shri Ajay Tamta, Cabinet Minister Textile, Member of Parliament (Almora) and appraised him about the historical background of Kanvashram and presented to him the book written by me **"कण्वाश्रम – चक्रवर्ती सम्राठ भरत की जन्मस्थली तथा भारतवर्ष की पौराणिक एवम एतिहासिक धरोहर".** The discussion was positive and the minister assured of all possible help in respect to the excavation to be undertaken in Kanvashram and in furthering the cause of the ancient heritage site.

Approval was accorded by the Director (Exploration & Excavation) ASI, New Delhi, **(Figure 26)** which directed the ASI, Circle Office, Dehradun to undertake the Trial Trench excavation in Kanvashram, to be completed by 30th September 2018. The letter also directed that a fortnightly report be submitted on the commencement of the excavation work. It was intimated by ASI, Circle Office Dehradun that the permission to carry out the excavation was not forthcoming from the Forest Department, Uttarakhand. Trial Trench excavation involved digging about four or five pits of area 2 x 2 m to a depth of about 2 or 3 m as required, to ascertain the presence of archaeological evidence, necessitating further excavation on a larger scale. The area where this excavation was to be undertaken is a bushy region with few trees. In any case, no trees were to be felled. Despite all this, the Forest Department, Uttarakhand did not grant permission to carry out Trial Trench excavation in the region. A period of six months was granted to complete the excavation work, to be completed by 30th September 2018.

Permission was not accorded by the Forest Department Uttarakhand and the granted excavation license lapsed. Efforts to get a fresh sanction to carry out excavation in Kanvashram did not materialize. However, with instructions from ASI, New Delhi office a team from ASI, Circle Office Dehradun arrived in Kanvashram on 4th January 2020. Once again, the archaeologist team went through the ritual of inspection of the site and gave a press briefing to the media. No further report or communication has since been received from ASI, New Delhi. The complete case of excavation in the Kanvashram region came to a dead end.

No.F.25/5/2017-EE
Government of India
Archaeological Survey of India

24 Tilak Marg, New Delhi-110001
Dated: March, 2018

19 MAR 2018

To

Superintending Archaeologist,
Archaeological Survey of India,
Dehradun Circle,
Dehradun

Sub:- Trial Trench Excavation at Kanvashram, near Kotdwar, District Pauri Garhwal, Uttarakhand during the season 2017-18.

Madam,

Please refer to your letter No.2/15/2016-EE/1107 dated 09.02.2018, I hereby convey the permission of the Director General, Archaeological Survey of India, as required under Para 12.9.1 of the Archaeological Works Code for conducting **Trial Trench Excavation at Kanvashram, near Kotdwar, District Pauri Garhwal, Uttarakhand.**

The Trial Trench Excavation would be conducted under the direction of **Smt. Lily Dhasmana, Superintending Archaeologist, Archaeological Survey of India, Dehradun Circle, Dehradun.**

The sanction is further subjected to the provisions of the Ancient Monuments and Archaeological Sites and Remains Act, 1958.

Necessary expenditure sanction may be obtained wherever required as per the Para 12.9.1 to 12.15 of Archaeological Work Code. **The approval is valid up to 30.9.2018.**

The Annual Interim Report of the work done comprising relevant section drawings, stratigraphy, and important findings with illustrations should be submitted immediately after completion of the work to this office. All antiquities found during the trial trench excavation will be documented and submitted in the format of National Mission on Monuments and Antiquities (NMMA), available at the website of NMMA (copy enclosed) immediately after the completion of trial trench excavation work. Fortnightly progress report shall also be submitted to this office positively after commencement of the work.

Excavation Report should be submitted as per Wheeler Committee Report 1965 – comprising the facts of the excavation, the plan of the site, its stratigraphy, the relationship of buildings and objects to the culture or cultures, a brief definition of these cultures in the light of present knowledge, a precise account of the work done should also be submitted before the next field season.

Yours faithfully,

(JitendraNath)
Director (Exploration & Excavation)

Copy to:

1. Smt. Lily Dhasmana, Superintending Archaeologist, Archaeological Survey of India, Dehradun Circle, Dehradun.
2. Regional Director, Northern Region, Archaeological Survey of India, Red Fort, Delhi.
3. F.No.2/1/2017-EE
4. Guard File

Fig 26 - Trail Trench Excavation Letter

EPILOGUE

Kanvashram is a place that symbolizes the very spirit and soul of this nation Bharat Varsh. For it was here that the human first understood and developed new insight into their own existence, in this vast universe. The fire of knowledge, which was kindled in the inhabitants, who lived on the bank of river Sarasvati, continued unabated. It is for this very reason that Sarasvati has been associated with education and knowledge, and was ultimately elevated to the highest pedestal, as Goddess of knowledge and worshipped till date. The Vedic culture, moulded out of the wisdom of migrants, ultimately matured on the bank of river Malini, under the aegis of rishis residing in and around Kanvashram. The light of knowledge generated by these rishis spread to the entire world. The essence of words spoken by the rishis were gathered and consolidated over hundreds of years. They were systematically composed into shloks and transmitted verbally from one generation to another. It is a miracle that after hundreds of years, the words of wisdom, uttered by the learned rishis continue to exist. The verses composed by different rishis and their descendants were fused and scripted, which formed the first written document called Rig Veda. Kanvashram, under rishi Kanv, as an educational centre, was the focal point of this complete transformation.

APPENDIX A

Prof. B.M. Khanduri
Head

Department of History/Ancient Indian History, Culture and Archaeology
H.N.B. Garhwal University
Srinagar Garhwal (Uttaranchl) - 246174
P.B. No. - 16
Fax : (01388) - 52217
Museum - 52389
Office - 52219
Lab. - 52093
Residence - 52416
e-mail : bmkhanduri@yahoo.com

अधीक्षण पुरातत्व विद्
भारतीय पुरातत्व सर्वेक्षण
आगरा मण्डल
२२- मालरोड़
आगरा - २८२००१

विषय : कण्वाश्रम (कोटद्वार) के उत्खनन के क्रम में।

महोदय,

आपके पत्रांक सं० ३/२४/६१-एच-६४७ दिनांक ८ नवम्बर २००२ के संदर्भ में आपको सूचित करना चाहता हूँ कि इतिहास एवं प्राचीन भारतीय इतिहास, संस्कृति तथा पुरातत्व विभाग ग०वि०वि० ने कण्वाश्रम, कोटद्वार में कोई भी उत्खनन् का कार्य नहीं किया है।

इस सम्बन्ध में मैं आपको सूचना देना चाहता हूं कि १९८९-९० में दैनिक अखबार अमर उजाला की रिपोर्ट के आधार पर विभाग से डॉ० प्रदीप सकलानी, डॉ० राजपाल सिंह नेगी तथा श्री जगदीप सिंह नेगी का तत्कालीन विभागाध्यक्ष प्रो० के०पी० नौटियाल ने विश्वविद्यालय के संग्रहालय के लिये इन मूर्तियों को लेने भेजा था। विभाग की इस टीम ने तत्कालीन प्रशासन तथा पुलिस अधीक्षक से वार्ता करके प्रशासन ने कण्वाश्रम से प्राप्त तीन पत्थर की मूर्तियां तथा दो स्तम्भ हमारे संग्रहालय को सौंपे थे। ये सभी मूर्तियां संग्रहालय में मूर्ति वीथिका में प्रदर्शित हैं। मूर्तियों का विवरण आपको पत्र के साथ संलग्न किया जा रहा है।

सधन्यवाद,

भवदीय
(बी० एम० खण्डूडी)
१४.११.२००१

पत्थर की मूर्तियों के नमूने

हिमालयी पुरातत्व एवं नवशीय संग्रहालय,
हे0न0ब0ग0वि0वि0, श्रीनगर गढ़वाल

कण्वाश्रम से प्राप्त मूर्तियों का विवरण - (   )

(१) गंगा, भारपुत्र व दो त्रिभंगी नृत्य पुरुष (स्तम्भ) १२वीं श०ई०

परिमाप :- ६६ सेमी० x १५ सेमी० x १४ सेमी० - कण्वाश्रम

विवरण :- गंगा दाहिने हाथ में घाट धारण किए हुए है। इसके ऊपरी भाग में दो-दो त्रिभंगी नृत्य पुरुष दिखाये गये हैं।

(२) **गणेश स्तम्भ १०वीं श०ई०**

परिमाप :- ६१ सेमी० x ३८ सेमी० x २५ सेमी० - कण्वाश्रम

विवरण :- प्रतिमा को द्विभुजी दिखाया गया है। दायें हाथ में दण्ड व बायें हाथ में मोदक धारक किये हुए हैं। मूर्ति को स्थानक मुद्रा में दिखाया गया है। प्रतिमा के ऊपर स्तूप की आकृति का अलंकरण किया गया है।

(३) **पार्वती १२वीं श०ई०**

परिमाप :- ५८ सेमी x २२ सेमी० x २०.५ सेमी - कण्वाश्रम

विवरण :- पार्वती को चतुर्भुजी दिखाया गया है। इनमें कमण्डल, खड्ग व गदा दिखाये गये हैं। नीचे के दायें हाथ को वरद मुद्रा में दिखाया गया है। मूर्ति के ऊपर स्तूप की आकृति का अलंकरण किया गया है।

(४) **पार्वती १०वीं श०ई०**

परिमाप :- ६८ सेमी० x १६ सेमी० x १८ सेमी - कण्वाश्रम

विवरण :- पार्वती को तपोवन में पाँच-पाँच अग्नि की ज्वालाओं के मध्य में तपस्या करते हुए दिखाया गया है। दायें व बायें एक-एक सिंह की आकृतियां उत्कीर्ण की गयी हैं।

(५) **कार्तिकेय १२वीं श०ई०**

परिमाप :- ५४.५ सेमी x ५१ सेमी० x २३ सेमी - कण्वाश्रम

विवरण :- कार्तिकेय की मूर्ति द्विभुजी है। एक में प्याला धारण किये हुए हैं व दूसरा खण्डित है। प्रतिमा के ऊपर दायें व बायें ओर कमल पुष्प वे बेल-बूटों का अलंकरण किया गया है। कार्तिकेय कुण्डल व हार धारण किये हुए हैं। सिर पर केश ऊपर की ओर सज्जित हैं जो कि पीछे की ओर एक गांठ में गुंथे गये हैं।

सधन्यवाद,

भवदीय

उप अधीक्षण पुरातत्वविद्

हिमालयी पुरातत्व एवं नृवशीय

६) **त्रिभंगी महिला प्रतिमा**

१२ वीं शताब्दी ई०

कण्वाश्रम

परिमाप :- लम्बाई ३० सेमी X चौ० २० सेमी० X मो० २० सेमी०

विवरण :- बलुए प्रस्तर स्तम्भ पर त्रिभंगी महिला मूर्ति अस्पष्ट मुख-मुख में गले में हार, अस्पष्ट कर्णाभूषण, दाहिने कंधे से बांह व बाजू के पीछे होते हुए लम्बा दुपट्टा हाथ से पकड़े हुए है, जो कि पैरों तक लटका हुआ है। कटि प्रदेश से पैरों तक धोती पहने हुए हैं तथा स्तन प्रदेश नग्न है। बाईं ओर का जंघ प्रदेश व हस्त खण्डित है।

७) **अस्पष्ट देव प्रतिमा**

१२वीं शताब्दी ई०

कण्वाश्रम

परिमाप :- ल० ३० सेमी X चौ० ३० सेमी० X मो० २८ सेमी०

विवरण :- बलुए प्रस्तर स्तम्भ पर तीन कमल की पंखुड़ियों के ऊपर अस्पष्ट खण्डित पशु की आकृति (स्तम्भवतः वृषभ) या अश्व उत्कीर्ण की गयी है। पशु आकृति के ऊपर एक देव-मूर्ति (दो पैरों वाली) उत्कीर्ण की गयी है जो कि बैठी अवस्था में दिखाया गया है। प्रतिमा का दायां पावं पशु के ऊपर अवलम्बित है। इस प्रतिमा की पहचान कर पाना कठिन है। क्योंकि प्रतिमा का सिर खण्डित है।

APPENDIX B

कार्यालय अधीक्षण पुरातत्त्वविद्
भारतीय पुरातत्त्व सर्वेक्षण
देहरादून मण्डल
'धरोहर', त्यागी रोड, देहरादून
उत्तराखण्ड – 248001
फैक्स / फोन: 0135 2628027
फोन: 0135 2723390

भारत सरकार
Govt. of India
सत्यमेव जयते

O/o Superintending Archaeologist
Archaeological Survey of India
Dehradun Circle
'Dharohar', Tyagi Road, Dehradun
Uttarakhand - 248001
Fax/Phone: 0135 -2628027
Phone: 0135-2723390
E mail- circledeh.asi @gmail.com

पत्र सं० Letter No. 2 / 69 / 2007–स्मा० 1043

दिनांक: Dated- 11.10.2012

सेवा में

महानिदेशक
भारतीय पुरातत्त्व सर्वेक्षण,
जनपथ नई दिल्ली –11

विषय: जनपद पौड़ी (उत्तराखण्ड) स्थित कोटद्वार नामक कस्बे के निकट स्थित कण्वाश्रम स्थल से प्रस्तर कलाकृतियों के प्रकाश मे आने एवं स्थल का निरीक्षण के सम्बन्ध में।

महोदय,

उपरोक्त के सन्दर्भ श्री वी0एस0 रावत, ले0 कमान्डर (से0नि0) द्वारा जनपद पौडी में स्थित कोटद्वार कस्बे के निकट स्थित कण्वाश्रम नामक स्थल से प्राप्त प्रस्तर कलाकृतियों के प्रकाश में आने एवं उक्त स्थल का निरीक्षण कराने का अनुरोध अपने ई मेल पत्र द्वारा महानिदेशक, भारतीय पुरातत्त्व सर्वेक्षण से किया गया था। महानिदेशक, भारतीय पुरातत्त्व सर्वेक्षण के पत्रांक दिनांक 27.07.12 के सन्दर्भ मे मण्डल कार्यालय की तकनीकी टीम ने अधीक्षण पुरातत्त्वविद के निर्देशन मे दिनांक 21.09.12 को उक्त स्थल का निरीक्षण किया जिसकी आख्या आपके सुलभ अवलोकनार्थ प्रेषित है।

भवदीय

संलग्नक: उपरोक्तानुसार।

ह०-

अधीक्षण पुरातत्त्वविद्

प्रतिलिपि –श्री वी0एस0 रावत, ले0 कमान्डर (से0नि0), पो0–कलालघाटी, कोटद्वार, जनपद–पौडी (उत्तराखण्ड) को सूचनार्थ।

अधीक्षण पुरातत्त्वविद्

कण्वाश्रम (जनपद पौड़ी) की निरीक्षण आख्या

श्री वी0एस0 रावत, ले0 कमान्डर (से0नि0) द्वारा महानिदेशक, भारतीय पुरातत्त्व सर्वेक्षण को जनपद पौडी में स्थित कोटद्वार नामक कस्बे के निकट स्थित कण्वाश्रम से प्राप्त प्रस्तर कलाकृतियों के प्रकाश में आने एवं उक्त स्थल का निरीक्षण कराने सम्बन्धी पत्र के क्रम में तथा महानिदेशक, भारतीय पुरातत्त्व सर्वेक्षण के पत्रांक दिनांक 27.07.12 के सन्दर्भ में मण्डल कार्यालय की तकनीकी टीम ने अधीक्षण पुरातत्त्वविद् के निर्देशन में दिनांक 21.09.12 को उक्त स्थल का निरीक्षण किया जिसकी आख्या निम्नलिखित है-

उत्तराखण्ड के तराई क्षेत्र कोटद्वार (जनपद पौडी) से देवी मन्दिर मार्ग पर 12 कि0मी0 दूर मालनी नदी के तट पर स्थित कण्वाश्रम नामक स्थल 29^{0} 47' 27" उत्तरी अक्षांश एवं 78^{0} 27' 08" पूर्वी देशान्तर के मध्य स्थित है। प्राचीन साहित्य में कण्वाश्रम का विवरण अनेक ग्रन्थों में मिलता है जिनमें ***महाभारत, स्कन्द पुराण*** एवं महाकवि ***कालीदास*** कृत अभिज्ञानशाकुन्तलम् प्रमुख हैं। महाकवि कालिदास ने अपने संस्कृत नाटक अभिज्ञानशाकुन्तलम्, जिसका सम्भावित कालक्रम गुप्त कालीन माना जाता है, में महार्षि कण्व का आश्रम मालनी नदी के तट पर वर्णित किया है। ज्ञातव्य है कि महाभारत कालीन राजा दुष्यन्त की पत्नी शकुन्तला जो कालीदास के नाटक की मुख्य पात्र है, का पालक पिता कण्व ऋषि को माना जाता है। कण्वाश्रम के मालनी नदी के तट पर स्थित होने के अन्य उदाहरण महाभारत एवं स्कन्दपुराण में भी मिलते हैं। डॉ0 परमानन्द मिश्र द्वारा 1889 में सम्पादित गढवाल-गजेटियर में उल्लिखित है कि कालीदास से पूर्व मौर्य काल में भारत आये यूनानी दूत मेगस्थनीज ने भी मालनी नदी का उल्लेख अपनी यात्रा विवरण में भी किया है। गंगा की सहायक नदी मालनी उत्तराखण्ड के पर्वतों से निकलती है तथा मैदानी क्षेत्र में यह नदी गंगा में मिल जाती है। मालनी नदी को पौराणिक राजा दुष्यन्त के काल से समीकृत माना गया है।

श्री वी0एस0 रावत, के अनुरोध का कारण हाल ही मे बरसात के कटाव से इस स्थल से निकली प्रस्तर मूर्तियाँ/शिलाएं है। डॉ0 पदमेश बुडाकोटी, निदेशक, हिमालयी धरोहर अध्ययन केन्द्र, कोटद्वार-गढवाल (उत्तराखण्ड) द्वारा उक्त सन्दर्भ में भेजे गये पत्र द्वारा अवगत कराया है कि समय-समय पर इस स्थल से अनेक कलाकृतियाँ प्रकाश में

आती रही तथा सन् 1991 में कण्वाश्रम स्थित मृग विहार के निकट बरसाती नाले द्वारा भूमि कटाव के कारण 36 प्रस्तर मूर्तियाँ/शिला पट्ट प्राप्त हुये।

मण्डल कार्यालय द्वारा किये गये स्थल निरीक्षण में पूर्व में प्राप्त उक्त मूर्तियां वर्तमान समय में प्राप्ति स्थल पर उपलब्ध नहीं है। निरीक्षणोपरान्त पाया गया कि यह स्थल वर्तमान में वन विभाग के अधिपत्य में है तथा टीले के कटाव वाले नाले-नुमा स्थल पर अनेक अलंकृत शिला पट्ट जिनमें यक्ष-यक्षी व मन्दिर निर्माण में प्रयुक्त किये जाने वाले उत्कीर्णित प्रस्तर खण्ड प्रकाश में आये हैं। वर्तमान में प्राप्त अलंकृत प्रस्तर खण्ड पूर्व में प्राप्त पुरावशेषों के शेष भाग ही हैं जिनमें कोई प्रमुख प्रतिमा पृथक रूप में प्राप्त न होकर उक्त शिला पट्टों पर ही उत्कीर्ण हैं जो प्राप्ति स्थल पर यत्र-तत्र अवस्थित हैं। अवलोकन से ज्ञात होता है कि पूर्व में प्रकाश में आये अलकृत प्रस्तर खण्डों का उपयोग वन विभाग द्वारा संरक्षित मृग विहार की चारदीवारी को निर्मित किये जाने में प्रमुखता से किया गया है तथा प्रमुख प्रतिमाओं को गढवाल विश्वविद्यालय द्वारा ले जाये जाने तथा तत्पश्चात हरिद्वार के किसी आश्रम को दिये जाने की सूचना स्थानीय व्यक्तियों द्वारा दी गयी। उक्त मूर्तियां इस समय कहां हैं यह ज्ञात नहीं है जिससे उनका अवलोकन हो सके कि वे किन देवी-देवताओं की हैं तथा उनकी निर्माण शैली क्या है जिससे उनके काल खण्ड का आकलन किया जा सके।

वर्तमान में इस स्थल से प्रकाश में आई कलाकृतियॉं/मूर्तियॉं/प्रतिमाऐं अलंकृत प्रस्तर खण्डों पर उत्कीर्णित हैं जिनमें किसी देवी-देवता की प्रमुख प्रतिमा नहीं है। प्राप्त अवशेषों में अन्य गौण देव मूर्तियों में से, एक यक्षी प्रतिमा उल्लेखनीय है जिसका शीर्ष भाग गधे के आकार का है। इस प्रकार की प्रतिमायें पूर्व में अन्य स्थलों सें भी प्राप्त हुई है जिनमें अलग-अलग पशुओं के मुखाकार निर्मित किये गये हैं तथा प्रतिमा शास्त्रीय अध्ययन के आधार पर इस प्रकार की मूर्तियों को यक्ष-यक्षी से सम्बद्ध किया जाता है। प्रकाश में आई अन्य मूर्तियॉं अस्पष्ट है जिनमे एक मानव मूर्ति है जो कि गोल आकार की ढालनुमा वस्तु लिये हुए खडी मुद्रा में उत्कीर्णित है।

इनके अतिरिक्त अन्य कोई महत्वपूर्ण प्रतिमाशास्त्री लक्षणों से युक्त मूर्तियां प्रकाश में नहीं आयी हैं। उपरोक्त मूर्तिया भी स्वतंत्र रूप में न होकर प्रस्तर शिला खण्डों पर अलकरणो के साथ उत्कीर्ण की गयी हैं। बहुतायत मात्रा में प्राप्त उक्त प्रस्तर शिला खण्ड किसी ध्वस्त प्राचीन मन्दिर/मन्दिरों के अवशेष हैं। ऐसा प्रतीत होता है कि प्राचीन काल में इस स्थल पर कोई मन्दिर अथवा लघु देवालय निर्मित रहे होंगे जिनके द्वार एवं पार्श्व के अवशेष इन अलंकृत शिला खण्डों के रूप मे प्रकाश में आये हैं!

उक्त पुरावशेष इस स्थल के पहाडी ढलान से मिलते हैं जो यहा के प्राचीन स्थापत्य निर्माण का सबसे निचला स्तर प्रतीत होता है तथा इसी नालेनुमा स्थल से लोहित मृणपात्र–खण्ड अल्प मात्रा में प्रकाश में आये हैं जो इस पुरास्थल के ऊपरी स्थल के कटाव के फलस्वरूप नीचे की ओर नाले में आये हैं। इनके अतिरिक्त यहां से अन्य कोई पुरावशेष दृष्टिगत नहीं होते। पुरास्थल के भोगौलिक परिदृश्य/परिपेक्ष को देखने से ऐसा प्रतीत होता है कि इस स्थल के समीप अथवा ऊपरी भाग में प्राचीन पुरास्थल/स्थापत्य निर्माण के प्रमाण होने की सम्भावना है। नाले में कटाव द्वारा लाये गये मृणपात्र खण्ड भी इस अवधारणा की पुष्टि करतें हैं। चूंकि उक्त स्थल दुर्गम वन एवं वनस्पतियों से आच्छादित है अतः उक्त पुरास्थल के वास्तविक विस्तार को ज्ञात कर पाना दुष्कर कार्य है तथापि स्थानीय व्यक्तियों तथा वन विभाग के अधिकारियों एवं कर्मचारियों के सहयोग से उक्त स्थल के मूल अथवा मुख्य भाग को खोजने हेतु पुर्न–अन्वेषण किया जाना समीचीन होगा तथा विस्तृत अन्वेषण द्वारा न केवल इस स्थल के पुरातात्त्विक महत्व एवं सांस्कृतिक गतिविधियों पर प्रकाश पडेगा अपितु उत्तराखण्ड के इस तराई क्षेत्र में प्राचीन संस्कृतियों का अनुक्रम भी ज्ञात हो सकेगा। अतः इस पूरे क्षेत्र का विस्तृत पुरातात्विक सर्वेक्षण/अन्वेषण करना आवश्यक है इससे पहाडी एवं तराई क्षेत्र में हुई परस्पर सांस्कृतिक गतिविधिया प्रकाश मे आ सकेंगी तथा इस क्षेत्र के प्राचीन इतिहास में नये आयाम जुड सकेंगे।

(अतुल भार्गव)
अधीक्षण पुरातत्वविद्

स्थल से प्राप्त अलंकृत प्रस्तर खण्ड

स्थल से प्राप्त अलंकृत प्रस्तर खण्ड

अलंकृत प्रस्तर खण्ड एवं स्थल से प्राप्त यक्षी प्रतिमा

गोल आकार की ढालनुमा वस्तु लिये हुए खडी मुद्रा में मानव मूर्ति

कण्वाश्रम, कोटद्वार (जनपद पौड़ी) उत्तराखण्ड, स्थल के छायाचित्र

प्रतिमा एवं प्रस्तर खण्ड प्राप्ति स्थल (बरसाती नाले) का सामान्य दृश्य

वन विभाग द्वारा निर्मित मृग विहार की चारदीवारी जिसमें स्थल से प्रकाश में आये प्रस्तर खण्डों का उपयोग किया गया है। (सामान्य दृश्य)

APPENDIX C

कण्वाश्रम क्षेत्र, कोटद्वार (जनपद पौड़ी) की निरीक्षण आख्या

निदेशक अन्वेषण एवं उत्खनन, भारतीय पुरातत्त्व सर्वेक्षण नई दिल्ली के पत्रांक 23/5/2017–अ0उ0(VIP) दिनांक 18.12.2017 के सन्दर्भ में मण्डल कार्यालय की तकनीकी टीम द्वारा अधोहस्ताक्षरी के निर्देशन में दिनांक 19.01.2018 को कण्वाश्रम क्षेत्र का निरीक्षण किया जिसकी आख्या निम्नलिखित है–

उत्तराखण्ड के तराई क्षेत्र कोटद्वार (जनपद पौड़ी गढ़वाल) से देवी मन्दिर मार्ग पर 12 कि0मी दूर मालिनी नदी के तट पर स्थित कण्वाश्रम नामक स्थल 29°47'27'' उत्तरी अक्षांश एवं 78°27'08'' पूर्वी देशान्तर के मध्य स्थित है। प्राचीन साहित्य में कण्वाश्रम का विवरण अनेक ग्रन्थों में मिलता है जिनमे ***स्कन्द पुराण*** एवं महाकवि ***कालीदास*** कृत अभिज्ञानशाकुन्तलम प्रमुख हैं। महाकवि कालिदास ने अपने संस्कृत नाटक अभिज्ञानशाकुन्तलम, जिसका सम्भावित कालक्रम गुप्त कालीन माना जाता है, में महार्षि कण्व का आश्रम मालिनी नदी के तट पर वर्णित किया है।

पूर्व में 2012 में ले0 कमाण्डर श्री वी0एस0 रावत निवासी कलाल घाटी, कोटद्वार के अनुरोध के क्रम में तत्कालीन अधीक्षण पुरातत्त्वविद् ने भी तकनीकी टीम के साथ स्थल निरीक्षण कर आख्या प्रस्तुत की थी जिसकी छायाप्रति संलग्नक के रूप में प्रेषित की जा रही है।

वर्तमान में निरीक्षण के दौरान पाया गया कि यह स्थल वन विभाग के अधिपत्य में है तथा टीले के कटाव वाले नाले–नुमा स्थल पर अनेक अलंकृत शिला पट्ट व मन्दिर निर्माण में प्रयुक्त किये जाने वाले उत्कीर्णित प्रस्तर खण्ड प्रकाश में आये हैं। वर्तमान में प्राप्त अलंकृत प्रस्तर खण्ड पूर्व में प्राप्त पुरावशेषों के शेष भाग ही है जिनमें कोई प्रमुख प्रतिमा पृथक रूप में प्राप्त न होकर उक्त शिला पट्टों पर ही उत्कीर्ण हैं जो प्राचीन स्थल पर यत्र–तत्र अवस्थित हैं। अवलोकन से ज्ञात होता है कि पूर्व में प्रकाश में आये अलंकृत प्रस्तर खण्डों का उपयोग वन विभाग द्वारा संरक्षित मृग विहार की चारदीवारी को निर्मित किये जाने में प्रमुखता से किया गया है तथा प्रमुख प्रतिमाओं को गढ़वाल विश्वविद्यालय के कर्मचारियों द्वारा तथा [illegible] वर्ष पूर्व वहां के प्रकाश मे आई प्रस्तर निर्मित [illegible] की प्रतिमा को हरिद्वार स्थित गुरुकुल कांगड़ी संग्रहालय ले जाया गया।

इस स्थल से प्रकाश में आई कलाकृतियॉ/मूर्तियॉं/प्रतिमाएँ अलंकृत प्रस्तर खण्डों पर उत्कीर्णित हैं उपरोक्त मूर्तियाँ स्वतंत्र रूप से न होकर प्ररतर शिला खण्डों पर अलंकरणों के साथ उत्कीर्ण की गयी हैं। बहुतायत मात्रा में प्राप्त प्ररतर शिला खण्ड किसी ध्वस्त प्राचीन मन्दिर/मन्दिरों के अवशेष हैं। ऐसा प्रतीत होता है कि प्राचीन काल में इस स्थल पर कोई मन्दिर अथवा लघु देवालय निर्मित रहे होंगे जिनके द्वार एवं पार्श्व के अवशेष इन अलंकृत शिला खण्डों के रूप में प्रकाश में आये हैं।

उक्त पुरावशेष इस स्थल के पहाडी ढलान से मिलते हैं जो यहां के प्राचीन स्थापत्य निर्माण का सबसे निचला स्तर प्रतीत होता है तथा इसी नालेनुमा स्थल से पूर्व में लोहित मृणपात्र–खण्ड अल्प मात्रा में प्रकाश में आये थे जिनके इस पुरास्थल के ऊपरी स्थल के कटाव के फलस्वरूप नीचे की ओर नाले में आने की संभावना है। पुरास्थल के भोगौलिक परिदृश्य/परिपेक्ष को देखने से ऐसा प्रतीत होता है कि इस स्थल के समीप अथवा ऊपरी भाग में प्राचीन पुरास्थल/स्थापत्य निर्माण के प्रमाण होने की संभावना है। स्थल के निरीक्षण के साथ सर्वेक्षण, टोटल स्टेशन के द्वारा विशेषज्ञो द्वारा किया गया। स्थल के प्राचीन प्रस्तर अवशेष, स्थापत्य निर्माण के नमूने एवं अन्य पुरावशेषों के प्रकाश में आने के इस स्थल के परीक्षण–उत्खनन की आवश्यकता है जिससे न केवल इस स्थल के पुरातात्त्विक महत्व एवं सांस्कृतिक गतिविधियों पर प्रकाश पड़ेगा अपितु उत्तराखण्ड के इस तराई क्षेत्र ने प्राचीन संस्कृतियों का अनुक्रम भी ज्ञात हो सकेगा तथा पहाडी एवं तराई क्षेत्र में हुई परस्पर सांस्कृतिक गतिविधियाँ प्रकाश में आ सकेंगी।

निरीक्षण आख्या छायाचित्रों एवं स्थल मानचित्र सहित कृपया सुलभ संज्ञान एवं परीक्षण उत्खनन (Trial Trench) की स्वीकृति हेतु प्रस्तुत है।

अधीक्षण पुरातत्त्वविद्

क्षेत्र से प्रकाश में आये अलंकृत प्रस्तर निर्मित पुरावशेष

देहरादून मण्डल कार्यालय की तकनीकी टीम द्वारा कण्वाश्रम क्षेत्र का स्थल निरीक्षण

CHRONOLOGY

Timeline of Kanvashram	
50 – 55 million	Present configuration of the continents took shape. Collision of Indian plate with Euro-Asian plate. Formation of the youngest mountain range Himalayas.
10 million years	Regular periodic cycle of monsoon rain commenced in the subcontinent.
20,000 BCE	Commencement of global warming and end of mini-Ice Age. Ocean level 120 metres lower than present day.
20,000 or earlier	Migration of humans from Africa to the Indian subcontinent.
11,500 BCE	Actual effective warming commenced.
10,000 BCE	Settlements established along the banks of river Sarasvati.
7500 BCE	Age of recently excavated settlement of Sarasvati – Sindhu civilisation.

6000 BCE	End of global warming. Ocean levels reached as seen today.
2700 BCE	Mature phase of Sarasvati – Sindhu civilisation.
2350 BCE to 1450 BCE	900 years of lean monsoon phase in the region. Reduction in flow of water in river Sarasvati.
2300 BCE	Commencement of disintegration of Sarasvati – Sindhu civilisation, due to reduction in flow of river Sarasvati Migration of settlers Northwards along the receding river Sarasvati and Eastwards towards Jamuna and Ganga.
1700 to -1600 BCE	Vedic civilisation/culture created by the migrants of the Sarasvati – Sindhu civilisation on the bank of river Malini. Establishment of Kanvashram. Birth of Emperor Bharat. Composition of Rig Veda shlokas by Rishis residing in and around Kanvashram.

1200 to - 1100 BCE	The great war -Mahabharat, fought in Kurukshetra between Pandavas and Kauravas, descendants of Emperor Bharat.
500 BCE	Scripting of epic Mahabharat.
1st century CE	Drama, Abhigyan Shakuntalam written by Kalidas, based on the events and happening in Kanvashram.
Aug 1955	Book, **शिवालिक की घाटियाँ में**, published by Shrinidhi Sidhantalankar, enumerating presence and importance of Kanvashram.
Feb 1956	Foundation stone of Kanvashram Memorial laid by Shri Jagmohan Singh Negi, Forest Minister, Uttar Pradesh, on Basant Panchami, on the left bank of river Malin, at Chawkighat, Kotdwara, Uttrakhand, indicating presence of Kanvashram.

Jul 2012	Relics and artifacts unearthed in Kanvashram. Findings reported to the Archaeological Survey of India, New Delhi. On four different occasions 2012, 2016, 2018 and 2020 ASI team carried out detailed surveys of the site.
Jan 2015	Book **"कण्वाश्रम – चक्रवर्ती सम्राठ भरत की जन्मस्थली तथा भारतवर्ष की पौराणिक एवम एतिहासिक धरोहर"** published by me.
May 2016	Kanvashram website www.kanvashram.org launched. Its Hindi translation uploaded 6 months later.
Nov 2017	Book "**Kanvashram- Birth Place of Emperor Bharat**" published by me.
Jun 2018	Kanvashram endorsed and recognised as an ancient heritage site. **Declared an ICONIC place**. Included in the 3rd list of ICONIC places issued by the Government of India.

GLOSSARY

Agni	-	Fire
Apsara	-	Fairy
Ashram	-	A place of residence of a rishi
Basant Panchami	-	A festival to honour Goddess Sarasvati
Bhabar	-	A region which lies at the foothills
Dhar	-	Lowest point on a mountain ridge
Dharma	-	A way of living
Ghandarv marriage	-	Marriage by mutual consent
Ghat	-	Place for cremation next to a river
Guru	-	Teacher or guide
Gurukul	-	An education institute
Havan kund	-	A fireplace to conduct religious rituals
Indra	-	Rain god
Mandal	-	Chapters
Nalla	-	a small stream
Rishi	-	A saint/sage

Sahita - Assimilation of assorted text
Sauti - A story teller
Shlok - a verse/hymn in Sanskrit
Vayu - Air
Yagya - A religious ritual

BIBILOGRAPHY

1. Rig Veda. *Translation Shriram Sharma and Bhagvati Devi Sharma*
2. Gita Press Gorakhpur. *Skhand Puran.*
3. Gita Gorakhpur Press. *Mahabharat (Hindi)*
4. Bibek Debroy. *The Mahabharata Vol 1, Penguin Random House, India*
5. Kalidas. *Abhigyan Shakuntalam*
6. Alexander Cunningham. *Ancient Geography India, Gyan Publishing House, New Delhi*
7. Michel Danino. *The Lost River, On the trail of the Sarasvati, Penguin Random House, India*
8. Shrinidhi Sidhantalankar. *Shivalik Ki Ghatio Me, Atma Ram and Sons, Delhi*
9. Shrinidhi Sidhantalankar. *Malini ke Vano Me, Atma Ram and Sons, Delhi*
10. S. Kalyanaraman. *Vedic River Sarasvati and Hindu Civilization, Aryan Book International, New Delhi*
11. Lalita Prasad. *Malini Sabhayata Ke Khander, Satyapath Prakashan, Kotdwar*

ACKNOWLEDGEMENT

I extend my gratitude to my daughter Vaishali for her meticulous handling of publishing related matters, to my son Vishal and daughter-in-law Mridul for their valuable assistance in cover design, and to my wife Vijaya for her unwavering support in coordinating and sustaining the team.

ABOUT THE AUTHOR

Lt. Commander Virendra Singh Rawat, post-retirement from Indian Navy, settled in his ancestral farm near Kotdwara, Pauri Garhwal, Uttarakhand. A graduate from National Defence Academy, (1970) he holds dual specialisation in Marine and Aeronautical Engineering. He resides close to the historic ancient heritage site Kanvashram, situated on the bank of River Malini, officially recognised in 1956 by the government of Uttar Pradesh, as birthplace of Emperor Bharat. Living in such a culturally rich environment inspired his deep interest in the area's history. Lt. Cdr. Virendra Singh Rawat is President of Kanvashram Vikas Samiti since 1998, an NGO, propagating the cause of heritage site. He is also credited with bringing to light to Archaeological Survey of India (ASI) the relics of ancient monuments unearthed in Kanvashram region in 2012. Due to his untiring efforts, in 2018 Kanvashram was included in the list of ICONIC places declared by Govt of India, to be glorified, under a scheme envisioned by the Honourable Prime Minister Shri Narendra Modi.

He is also playing a significant role in community development, educating and guiding children of the surrounding villages and training them in various sports disciplines like Basketball, Badminton, Lawn Tennis, Hockey etc. His dedication to both national service and grassroots social work reflects his commitment to holistic development and cultural preservation. He is also actively involved in welfare activities of veterans through various Ex-servicemen organisations since 1994.